WHO HIJACKED MY FAIRY TALE?

KELLY SWANSON

WHO HIJACKED My Fairy Tale?

How To Hang On To Humor When
Life Doesn't Go The Way You Planned!

KELLY SWANSON

Who Hijacked My Fairy Tale?

Copyright © 2009 by Kelly Swanson

Note: This book is a combination of fiction and non-fiction. The messages are true, the stories highly embellished. The names of the fictitious people have been changed to protect the innocent. The town of Cedar Grove is not to be confused with any existing Cedar Grove – any similarities are purely coincidental. Do not bring me on a talk show and rake me over the coals because I used my wacky cast of characters to deliver very valid points. Surely you have better things to do.

TABLE OF CONTENTS...

My Yellow Brick Road Was Filled With Potholes

My journey to the funny side of life

I was the kid they threw things at on the bus: the overweight girl who prayed nobody would notice her—the teenager with secret dreams of being more than the potted plant stuck at stage right. On the ladder of popularity I was somewhere in the next room asking where they put the ladder. For me, humor started as my defense mechanism—my way of coping in this world that fit me like a coat two sizes too small. I learned early in life that no matter how bad it got, there was always something to look forward to. I could find a way to be happy despite it all.

When I went away to college, I began to come out of my comfort zone, thanks to '80s dance music, nickel draft, and a dorm full of kids who helped me redefine normal. And my sense of humor came out of the closet. I could make people laugh, and the rush was like no other. Humor attracted friends: the potted plant had graduated to a coat rack. I was finally on the ladder of popularity. Granted, it was a footstool, but I had learned to take what I could get.

When I entered the real world and all of its real responsibilities and hardships, humor became my way of battling the bumps and knocks in the road. I had learned that no matter what happens, you always have a choice in how situations affect you. You can still find a way to smile through the pain, and I still hang on to that truth today.

Who would have guessed that I would end up making a living using my sense of humor? My job is making other people happy. Pinch me because it's too good to be true. But here I am. There are a lot of people out there who need to laugh, so job security is good.

That brings me to the reason I'm writing this book: to share with you the things that I have learned that help me stay on the funny side of life. You will quickly see that staying on the funny side of life isn't about writing jokes—or even being funny—but about the ability to see beyond your obstacles. This book is about attitude and how to work your way back to a healthy one, so that you can find a way to smile when life is anything but funny. In this book we dispel the fairy-tale myths that we are carrying around. We learn that the biggest obstacle standing in the way of our happiness is us. Humor isn't reserved for those who are born with it. Humor is for all of us—for those moments when life gets too serious or when the pain starts to overwhelm us. Humor reminds us that we're going to be okay—that we're still standing and we can still find something to laugh about. Humor is a gift. Don't leave yours unwrapped.

Kelly Swanson

Some day my prince will come
Some day I'll find true love
And how thrilling that moment will be
When the love of my life says to me
"You're not exactly what I'd pictured."

When you wish upon a star
Makes no difference who you are
Anything your heart desires
Will come to you
If you have the money

Somewhere over the rainbow skies are blue
And the dreams that you dare to dream really do come true
IF
You just take this little pill
Just one more sip why don't you, you will find it

Yes, you can be like Goldilocks
With just a dose of this botox
Why don't you find it
Yes, you can be the very best
With this new car and pair of breasts

You don't need money, just this card
To look much richer than you are
Your happiness it will begin
Well, as soon as you are thin
Your charming prince comes riding in
Don't like him? Hey, just trade him in
Somewhere over the rainbow way up high
There's a land that I heard of once in a lullaby
kcs

Who Hijacked My Fairy Tale?

What happened to my happily-ever-after

We live in a world that says you can have it all, you can have it now, and you can have it supersized. And I have yet to meet anyone whose life is going according to plan. Why are so many of us unhappy? Why is depression at an all-time high? Why are so many people struggling for life balance: stressed, burned out, trying to wear all these hats and feeling like none of them fit—trying to do it all and still feeling like they just don't measure up? We live in a world of opportunity, yet so many of us are living as if we're just waiting for that other shoe to drop. Why are so many of us living in survival mode? What ever happened to that fairy tale we were promised as children?

I, like most little girls, was raised on the fairy-tale formula: the concept that our lives should play out like a fairy tale—that we are little princesses existing in torment, singing under water, scrubbing fireplaces, or lying comatose under the spell of yet another evil stepmother, awaiting the arrival of our charming prince, whereupon life will begin and we will live happily-ever-after. The idea that we are trapped in this dismal existence until three furry little creatures come along and help us find our way out.

I have nothing against charming princes or the pursuit of happiness or furry creatures. But I do have a problem with teaching our children—and believing ourselves—that we are entitled to a happily-ever-after life, when the truth of the matter is that it doesn't exist. Somewhere along the way we all come to find that next page ripped out of our fairy tale—the scenery changed, the ending rewritten until it looks nothing like we had originally planned. Case in point: Derk McDermott, the charming prince of my high-school fairy tale.

You didn't know Derk, but I'd bet you knew somebody like him: good-looking, had money, got all the girls. Derk never looked at me once, and after we graduated he married the head cheerleader and they moved away to some big city and started having children with expensive names. Fifteen years later they split, he moved back, and just hearing that he was in town put me immediately back under his spell. Maybe, just maybe, this was my chance to be with the man of my dreams. Maybe he was tired of the hot-cheerleader type and was now looking for the chunky girl with the good personality. And he would take one look at me (I'd be wearing the jeans that make my butt look small) and ask where I'd been hiding all my life. Then he'd whisk me away (do men still whisk?) just like one of those made-for-TV movies starring Valerie Bertinelli. When I ran into his sister at the mall and she insisted she'd have him call me, I swear I could literally hear the flapping of the bluebirds' wings who were now gathering over my head to sew pearls on my ball gown.

This was the message I heard on my machine later that day: "Hey, it's Derk. Want to come over?" That was the message I played for my friends, neighbors, and the pizza guy who agreed it was a very good sign. I quickly ordered a subscription to *Brides 'R Us* Magazine, accepted the invitation, and ran out the door to go claim my charming prince and live happily-ever-after. That didn't exactly go the way I planned. I'll meet you back here in a minute.

My entire life has been an example of things not going the way I planned—or the way other people had planned, either. In case you can't tell from my accent, I am from the South—Georgia originally, born and raised. I've still got people down there, in Smyrna, Marietta, Atlanta, Cell Block D. Then I shamed them all and moved up *north* (spoken in a shocked whisper with a curled lip) to North Carolina. I come from a place where we're known for our grits, hospitality, and spray-painted marriage proposals. It's a place where some of us keep our sofas on the front porch, refrigerators in the garage, extra toilets out back, cars up on blocks, and where we think fine art is a set of those plastic geese scattered out in the front yard. We spend our Saturday mornings roaming flea markets trying to find one more set of ceramic pig salt-and-pepper shakers.

Where I come from you can be kissing your cousin, dragging a flatbed full of illegitimate children, and spending your weekends on one of those communes, naked, holding hands and chanting "Kumbaya"—and honey, we'll pray for you just the same. But bring a box of instant mashed potatoes to a family reunion and the women are going to shun you for three generations. Seriously, we'll help you cook, help paint your house, help birth your children—but you take our seat in church, and you are going down.

Where I come from, you can say anything about anybody as long as you start it off with a "well-you-know-I-don't-mean-to-be-ugly," throw in a couple of "well-I'm-just-sayings," and wrap it up with a "bless-your-heart." For instance: *Is that Mabel Jenkins out yonder? Well, you know I don't mean to be ugly. But get a look at that rear end. If that thing gets any bigger, to sit down she's gonna need some landing gear. Looks like her hips are in parentheses* (pause here and scrunch face up in pity). *Bless her heart.*

I come from a place where, for many of us, our futures had already been determined, either by the world or by the long line of well-meaning relatives hell-bent on making sure we didn't repeat their past mistakes. I grew up knowing exactly what was expected of me, as if it had been written on the walls. I would graduate high school with no tattoos and no babies; go to college; find a job that would pay the bills, nothing fancy; live close to home; and wait for my charming prince to come riding up, whereupon I would step into the quintessential role of wife and mother and live happily-ever-after. There was just one problem: No charming prince came riding up on a white horse to save me—nobody pledging his undying love, unless you count the tipsy guy swaying behind the Taste 'n Freeze and that probably doesn't count. Besides, he never called. When you're overweight and addicted to blue eye shadow, the charming princes aren't exactly lining up outside your door. At least that's what I told myself.

There was also another problem, in that I had one foot in the expected world (here's what you wear, here's what you drive, here's where you go on Friday nights, here's where you go to church, and here's how you worship) and another foot in this whole other world of passions and dreams. In this other world writing consumed me, and I was starting to fall in love with a wacky cast of characters who came alive on the page and talked inside my head, sometimes all at once.

In this world the shy kid who never fit in wanted to get up on stage and tell stories and make people laugh.

I think many people have this whole "other" world; they just keep it in a box on a high shelf and every now and then, or when they retire, they take it down, dust it off, and look at it. But for me, this other world kept getting bigger and bigger, and the real world smaller and smaller, until I found myself standing on a cliff surrounded by all those voices saying, "No, you can't do that," and that one tiny voice that said, "Oh yes, you can." And I jumped. And I never looked back. Okay, sometimes I look back, not in regret, but in awe of how close I came to never having jumped at all.

Maybe you're standing there on that cliff holding that box of dreams, scared to jump because you're surrounded by voices telling you that it can't be done. If that's the case, then let me be that one tiny voice telling you, "Yes, you can," and reminding you that often in life it isn't what we have or what we know that holds us back, but fear of falling. The most successful dreamers out there aren't the most talented or the luckiest, but the most persistent and the most courageous—the ones who were told they couldn't do it, and did it anyway. And here's a little secret: It's not the landing that's so much fun, but the time you spend in midair.

I've made many jumps in my life: the jump into faith, the jump into marriage, the jump into parenting, and the jump into the world of professional storytelling. Yes, you heard me right. I quit my job in the family business to become a professional storyteller—to make a living finding people to pay me to come and tell stories. Had I known how crazy it was, well, I probably would have done it anyway. You're talking to somebody who once wore purple leg warmers with silver threads woven in and a matching headband.

I started marketing myself as a professional storyteller to a world that had no idea what to do with me. Be a comedian—they know where to put you. Be a musician, be an actor—they know what to do with you. Be a professional storyteller and people say, "Oh...isn't that nice." And they give you that look that says they're not sure whether to congratulate you or pet you. It's the same look I got from my father when I quit the family business to go tell stories for a living. He's a loving man. He didn't say anything negative. He just got that look—that look that said, "Bless your heart. You're an idiot."

My mother wasn't much better. She said, "I don't know what to tell people you do."

I said, "Good grief, let's put this in perspective. My sister has an aerial view of Graceland tattooed on her back. My brother thinks that Bin Laden is posing as his shift supervisor over at the Golden Burger Barn. And *I'm* the disappointment?"

"Quit being so dramatic," she tells me. "You don't even have a brother."

It makes perfect sense to me that I would be a storyteller. I'm in love with stories and my characters. I'd rather write than do anything, except eat chocolate. I love to talk (just ask my husband), and I believe in the power of words—the words we tell ourselves, and the words we tell others. Your success in business and in life, in my humble opinion, can be traced back to your effective use of words.

Anyway, instead of taking the expected road, I chose to be a professional storyteller in a world that had already decided that did not fit into the box they had created, even the one labeled "Eccentric

Artists." It's okay. I was used to it. In some way or another, I have always been the proverbial piece that didn't fit. Let's go back again to my teen years when I wanted to dance.

Now, I'll admit, this was a long time ago, back before students started dating their teachers. Shoot, I was afraid to ask to sharpen my pencil, much less make a move. And our teachers weren't hot back then either. They were tired, old, bitter people that smelled like moss and cough drops, with skin the color of a dead chicken, and moles with hair growing so long you could trip over them.

Back then I wanted a "Members Only" jacket, the kind that actually said MEMBERS ONLY on it. But did I get it? No. I get a windbreaker my uncle Frank died in. Smelled like Jack Daniels and had a cigarette burn in the arm. I wanted to go to the beach for spring break, but no, I had to work over at Sunny Side Hills holding Uncle Edsel's teeth while he shouted *bingo!* and I had flashbacks of Enema Day. I wanted a Corvette with leopard-print seat covers and a coconut air freshener. But did I get it? No. I got my Uncle Nester's hand-me-down Dodge Dart that smelled like feet. The bumper was hanging off. It was held on by duct tape. It had a sticker on it that said, "Start a movement. Eat a prune." You try to be cool.

But I got it into my head that I wanted to dance. No thanks to my sister, who said, "You have got to be kidding. You run across the street and it takes your rear end an extra day just to catch up." But what did they know? When I danced, I felt free. When I danced, I felt beautiful. When I danced, people called 911. Widow Jenkins asked me was I having a seizure. They put a glass jar up in the convenience store with my picture on it asking for donations. But what did they know? I was good. They just didn't know talent when they saw it.

I decided that the best place for my newfound talent to manifest itself was going to be cheerleading tryouts. I know: I wasn't the brightest bulb in the pack. I was convinced that they would see my original dance moves and ask where I'd been hiding all this time, and hoist me on their shoulders and make me head cheerleader, and I would be popular at last. Well, cheerleading tryouts did not exactly go the way I'd planned. How did I know? Let's just say that the laughter was a pretty good indication. Not just behind-my-back polite twitters either, but in-my–face, side-splitting guffaws of laughter from that row of perky cheerleaders with the ironed-out hair. They were laughing so hard they couldn't breathe. Every head was thrown back so all I could see was this row of nostril tunnels and dangling tonsils.

It was by far the worst day of my childhood. I still remember my mother telling me I had to go back to school when I handed her my application for *Ladies of Grace Home for Unwed Mothers*. She said they would have forgotten all about it by then. WRONG. They hadn't forgotten about it. Every time I turned another corner I'd see someone mocking one of my original dance combinations, flailing on the floor like he was having a seizure, except for Harvey—his was for real, but he turned out to be okay.

That was the day I learned that I couldn't dance. But you know what? If I'd known then what I know now, I would have danced anyway. And sometimes even now, late at night, when everybody's asleep and the doors are locked and the shades are drawn, I'll turn on that music, and I'll dance. And sometimes I don't care what anybody says; sometimes I am really, really good.

Even though that was the day I learned I couldn't dance, it was also the day I learned that I could make people laugh. And as it turns out, I like that even more than dancing. And I started to appreciate the importance of humor and staying on the funny side of life. I had no idea how that ability would become more than just a good habit: a tool that would actually carry me through the toughest times in life. And I know that some of you are reading this and nodding your head, because I've met you: the ones who come up after my shows and tell me how you are living with cancer, losing your business, taking care of ill parents, and that the only way you get through it is through laughter. And if this isn't you, then it's time you get your head in the game.

My charming prince finally did come along, much later than I'd expected, and nothing like the order I'd put in for him—even better actually. I tell you, opposites attract, because that man is a genius. He lays awake at night pondering the mysteries of the universe. I lay awake at night wondering what happens to their tattoos when fat people lose weight. Don't be hating me for saying "fat" either, because I'm carrying enough extra pounds for the both of us, so I'm allowed.

My husband and I are at that stage of marriage that those fairy tales never told you about—that next chapter, the part where the honeymoon has ended, real life has set in, and you've got a pretty good idea of what forever is going to feel like. Where the charming prince has grown a spare tire, the princess has developed anger issues, and your dream of rocking on the front porch into the twilight of your life turns into unpaid bills, dirty laundry, and dreams of killing him in his sleep. Where the all-night hanky-panky turns into "Come on, babe, we've got five minutes before *Law and Order* starts." Where you go from wearing the lacy lingerie and saying, "Baby, come rub lotion on my shoulders," to "Come here, babe, look! You've got to see what's growing in between my toes! I think it's infected!"

Seriously, we work really hard at our marriage. We have a date night every week: he takes Mondays, and I take Thursdays. It's working out really well. But we still have our issues, like the other day when I told him that it had been a week since we'd really talked. He said, "Shoot, babe, I didn't want to interrupt."

Yeah, there's no question about it: marriage isn't what you think it's going to be. But nothing ever is. Marriage, just like life, doesn't promise a happily-ever-after, and the sooner you accept that and embrace it, the happier you'll be. I think the reason that so many marriages don't last is because people have an unrealistic idea of what it should be. They're hanging on to a fairy tale. And the sad thing is that there just might be a happily-ever-after if you know where to look. That's what we are going to talk about today (or next week if you're a slow reader): where to look to find your way back to happy.

As soon as I got married, I started trying for baby number one. I was so far behind the game (that means older) that my biological clock was the kind you still wind by hand. The plan was for me to have as many children as I could possibly have before my ovaries dried up. I got pregnant right away and started wearing maternity clothes the day I found out. Then I lost the baby. And I lost four more after that. This was definitely not in the fairy tale. Those were some dark times in my life, but oddly enough, they didn't feel as dark as they should have because I laughed my way through it. That's right. I laughed my way through it. No, it wasn't funny. Yes, I was sad. Really sad. So sad that I knew if I let myself "go there" I would never come back. And I made a choice. The situation was what it was. Nothing was going to change that. I had two options: to go through it crying, or to go through it laughing. I chose a third: to go through it laughing with some tears mixed in.

I still remember my friends asking me why I was so happy. I know they were whispering behind my back with words like "therapy" and "mental institution" and "this just isn't healthy for her to deal with her pain like this" and "good grief when did her butt get so big?" But they were wrong. It was the healthiest thing in the world. I faced my grief and then found my way out of it, over and over and over again. I chose to let the pain in for a limited amount of time, and then when I had grieved and let go of what I couldn't control, I would let the laughter in. I faced the fact that this dream may not come true, and if it didn't, I would be perfectly okay with that, and just find another dream. As long as I could laugh I was strong enough to try again. And I did. Until finally it stuck. And the sixth pregnancy was successful to the surprise of the doctors who could not explain it. And so, with a renewed appreciation for humor, and a faith that was now stronger than it had ever been thanks to this experience—yes, I said thanks to this experience—I charged full speed ahead into mommy-hood.

If you're reading my story with a heart that has lived it, then please hear me when I say that I am not making light of your pain. It is real, and you are allowed to grieve and mourn. It's part of the process. But at some point you have to get over it. At some point you have to find something bigger to hang on to. What will happen will happen despite your greatest effort to stop it. Sometimes the only choice you have is whether to go through it crying or laughing. And trust me: laughing is much better—and healthier too.

So now I'm a mommy who's intent on being the perfect parent. Yeah, well, that's not exactly going the way I'd planned either. In my defense, parenting is a lot harder than it looks, and a lot has changed since we were kids!

Now they have these *Mommy and Me* classes where you take your baby and go play. When I was growing up we didn't go to class with our mommies. We sat around and watched soap operas through the playpen bars. I was three years old before I realized the TV didn't have lines in it. Today they play with expensive video games. We played with barely rinsed-out tuna fish cans with lids sharp enough to lose a finger. They play Xbox; we played "Who's the first to get salmonella?" They have fancy concerts on ice. Do you know what we did for entertainment? We sat around on Sunday afternoons in hot living rooms staring at each other and watching Uncle Edsel pop out his teeth in between verses of "Keep on the Sunny Side."

And when kids get in trouble today, they get "time-out": the No-No chair. Isn't that special? I don't know about you, but where I come from, when we got into trouble in my neighborhood we got spanked hard—in the front yard—by somebody else's mamma! It was an unspoken rule that a mamma could spank any kid on her property that was misbehaving. That's why we never played over at Jimmy Van Cuso's house. His mamma could draw blood and not even spill her drink.

Depending on who you asked, the tools of torture, as we called them, varied: from the belt, to the switch (pick your own switch off the bush), to the pair of old faded flip-flops. In our house they were more culinary in nature: the wooden spoon, the spatula, the waffle iron. Sometimes Mom would make an exception and we'd get the plastic pink hairbrush. My mother could do damage with hair products, and being as I was what they would now call ADD—back then you were just a demon seed—I was on familiar terms with that hairbrush. I spent the majority of my youth with the word GOODY tattooed on my rear end. Mom would spank you with that thing until it broke, and then blame you for it. *Now look what you made me do.* Plastic pink hairbrush. It's no wonder I can't walk down the hair aisle of the Supermart without curling up in the fetal position.

Kids today don't believe me when I tell them we used to get paddled in school by the principal, Mr. Butkus. Remember those paddles with the holes drilled in them? And how they'd slide into the paddle holder on the back of the chair? Remember the sound? The sound of the *whack* of the wooden paddle up against the denim-clad rear end. And how that sound would travel. It would travel down hallways, bounce across lockers, and float two stories up and into that open window where we sat in music composition class singing, "Mine eyes hath seen the glory," knowing full well that Jimmy Van Cuso had been caught in the girls' locker room again and a paddling was near at hand. *Mine eyes hath seen the glory—WHACK!—of the coming of the Lord. WHACK!* To this day, I can't hear that song without clinching my butt cheeks in honor of Jimmy Van Cuso.

Yeah, a lot has changed since we were kids, and sometimes that scares me to death: the idea of putting my child out there in a world where morals and values are no longer universal, where truth has become relative to the person applying it. How can I be a parent in the face of such change? By having something bigger to hold on to—truths that never change. Change is necessary, and sometimes change can actually be good. But when you change without a strong unwavering vision, you stand for nothing but the next change to come your way. Many times in our life the obstacle blocking our path is change—change from what we think life is supposed to be like. So I'm living proof that the concept of a happily-ever-after life is unrealistic. It doesn't exist. Life never goes the way we planned. And the people said, "Amen."

At this point you're probably depressed and thinking that I'm the worst motivational speaker you've ever heard. *When God closes a door, He opens a window—so you can jump!* I don't mean to depress you, but the truth is the truth, and you have to face the mountain before you can climb it. And I promise—the goal of this book is not to depress you and rain on your dreams. Dreams are great. Dreams are necessary. The bigger the dream the better. And I will dream until I take my very last breath. I just believe that it is my calling to come and meet you in those moments when the dream has not gone the way you planned—when you find the next page of your fairy tale has just been ripped out, the scenery's changed, and the ending has been rewritten to where it looks nothing like you originally planned.

Sometimes I feel like Rocky in one of his movies. Pick any one and go to that scene where he's in the big fight and it's all come down to this, and he's been hit so many times you don't think he's going to get back up. And his face is all swollen and bloody and sweat is flying and the rest of the world is running in slow motion. And he's got one knee up and one knee down and his vision is blurring and his life is flashing before his eyes. And you're sitting on the edge of your seat whispering, "Come on, Rocky. You can do it. Get back up. Look how far you've come. Keep your eye on the prize. Dust yourself off and get back up."

For me, life is like that sometimes. Sometimes I am at the top of my game—high five over the tennis court net. And other times, more times than not, I'm hovering. I've got one knee down and one knee up, and I'm wondering how many times I'm going to be hit before I just can't get back up. And it's here, in these moments, where I have to find the strength to keep going. It's in these moments that I call on my God (that's another book) and my sense of humor. Not the ability to jump up and have a joke ready, or to run through the room with a rubber chicken, but the ability to find a way to smile when life is anything but funny. To remember that true victory—faith, success, character; whatever you want to call it—isn't cultivated in those moments when you cross the finish line, but in every one of those moments when you fall down, dust yourself off, and have the courage to get back up. That's where it matters. That's the true test. Happily-ever-after does not exist unless you know where to look—unless you're willing to find a new happy ending. Today I'm going to show you where to look. So let's not waste any more time. Your happy ending is waiting.

Myth #1 The Superhero

You are not one—and neither is your spouse

My son is convinced that he wants to be a superhero when he grows up: to scale tall buildings with a single leap, to decimate his enemies (yes, he uses the word *decimate*—thank you, television crime shows), and to wear a full-body leotard with the eyes cut out. The other day he got his head stuck in the grocery cart. I told him his chances were slim, and that if his father ever caught him wearing a full-body leotard he'd better be able to make a fast getaway. And that you can never become a superhero when you insist on eating nothing but corn dogs and popsicles. And the last time anyone scaled a building in this city he was wearing his underwear and a knit cap.

I remember in third grade I was convinced that Mr. Cox was Superman. It all added up. He had the dark glasses, the chiseled jaw, and even ran the school newspaper. And when he looked at me and told me I was a good writer, I was convinced that he was seeing through the pudgy kid in leg warmers to his beloved Lois Lane. And he always managed to show up when the other kids were picking on me, and if that didn't spell superhero, I don't know what did. And then one day Mr. Cox was gone. They didn't tell us why, but I could hear the whispered words spoken over our heads—words like "third offense" and "under the influence" and "the school has a reputation to protect." My beloved Superman was replaced with a substitute who smelled like moth balls and kept clearing her throat like a cat with a hair ball. Apparently Mr. Cox had become a bad man whose name could only be spoken in a whisper. But Mr. Cox was the one who always came to my defense when the other kids picked on me. Mr. Cox was the one who looked me in the eye and told me that suffering builds character and I had character. Mr. Cox was the only one who saw my potential. No, he wasn't Superman. He was even better.

We live in a world that bombards us with images and messages of who we should be, what we should look like, what we should own to be considered successful. We live in a world that tells us we can have it all and do it all. We live in a world that says, "One is not enough." That it's all about being the best, being on top, being noticed. You are nothing if you are average.

Have you seen the commercial for the kids' allergy medication? Two women are sitting in a park on a play date when one child runs up, sneezes, and both women, like gunslingers, pull out their emergency mommy medication. One mother has an oozing bag of mangled medications. The other mother pulls out her handy-dandy prefilled dose of medication and administers it to Junior and never misses a beat. Messy bag woman cowers in shame. Quick-dose mom flashes a condescending smile of victory. Freeze the frame right here because I have a problem with this whole scenario.

First of all, find me a park where children are frolicking and skipping to the tune of laughing mothers. Last park I went to, one kid peed on the slide, another bit his sister in the face, somebody found a hypodermic needle in the sand box, and my car got spray-painted with gang graffiti before I even turned off the engine. And it's not just moms anymore. I saw two dads, a grandparent, a babysitter, a kid who was thrown out the door of a station wagon as the parents 'rolled through,' another who I'm pretty sure lives there, and one man in slippers shuffling through the parking lot talking to himself. And who even has time for play dates anymore? I'm busy. My kid gets his play dates in line at the grocery store.

The TV moms are immaculately dressed. No wrinkles, no stains. Right now I'm wearing a T-shirt with crusted peanut butter and matching sweats that I've been wearing since Tuesday. I once went a whole day with a sucker stuck to the side of my head before anybody told me. The TV moms are chatting happily. Wrong. Sara's telling Sue about how lazy her husband is, while Bertha (who just slipped vodka into her water bottle) is complaining about how far her butt has dropped, but Erma can't hear her because she's too busy spanking her kid in the parking lot.

The commercial mothers are always deep in conversation while their kids are playing out on the horizon. Hello! Do you watch *Law and Order?* My child once disappeared behind a bush for a second and I started screaming, clawing at my sweater, and profiling the other moms. And what's up with the kid who comes up to his mother to sneeze? Please. My son can be bleeding out his eyes and he won't stop digging to come get help. Commercial mom whips out her bag of medications. We went on vacation and I forgot Junior's inhaler. She reaches into her purse and locates the bag of medicine immediately. I once went into my purse for a band aid—dug up four half-eaten candy bars, a pair of underwear, and a dead gerbil. No band aid.

Commercial kid takes his medication with a smile. I have to wrestle my kid to the ground, hold his nose, and threaten to take away Christmas if he doesn't take it. Commercial kid smiles and gives a cute, toothless "thank you" while my kid seeks vengeance with a Magic Marker on the living-room wall. Then Patty Perfect gives Susie Slack a condescending smile of victory. Well, I must admit, that one is pretty much on target. I've met Patty Perfect before. She's the one who frowns when I bring chocolate when it's my turn for preschool snack. When I put diet cola in his sippy cup. When I breastfeed at the salad bar.

Yeah—all that from a commercial. I'll probably still buy it anyway. It does look cool. I'm sure it will cost three times as much, I'll leave it at home, and my kid still won't take it. So maybe the commercial wins after all. But I won't let them tell me what normal mothers look like. Or what beautiful looks like either. Or success. Or happiness. What do they know?

We constantly strive to be more, have more, do more, and attain a higher standard of living. No wonder we're burned out. No wonder "life balance" is a hot topic these days. No wonder we're feeling like we don't measure up. No wonder we're never happy with what we've got. No wonder we feel let down by those on whom we continually place our high expectations. We're trying to be superheroes. And superheroes aren't real. They don't exist. So stop trying to be one, and stop trying to turn other people into superheroes.

You can't do everything. You can't fix everything. So quit trying. When you try to do everything right, you end up doing nothing right.

It's time that we stopped listening to the world. It's time to stop letting them define success, happiness, marriage, beauty, truth. We're not here to please the world. It's impossible. Let go of those unrealistic expectations that you carry around with you of how life should be and how people should be. The harder you hang on to this idea of the way things should be, the harder you will fall when—not if, but *when*—your expectations are not met. So how do we do this? Well, it's more of an ongoing process than a one-time checklist. But here are some points to help you shed the superhero mentality.

- Release unrealistic expectations

- Assess what you can realistically control

- Let go of what is out of your control

- Ask for help (it doesn't mean you're weak)

Discussion Questions:

1. Is there an area of your life or a current situation that is adding stress to your life? *(For example: I struggle with the fact that I can't keep my house clean. I am not afraid of dying in a car accident. I'm afraid that after I'm gone, people will go there and see that my floors aren't clean.)*

2. Are you carrying around an unrealistic expectation of how this situation should play out, or how somebody else

should be? Who are you trying to please? On the list of what you consider to be important priorities in life, is this one of them? In other words, when you are standing at the end of your life looking back, will this matter? Look back on the past year. What do you regret? *(Example: I feel bad about not having clean floors because I think that other mothers have clean floors. It doesn't bother me, but my mother always had clean floors. She would be disappointed. No, this is not a great priority in my life or I would probably be doing it. At the end of my life, it won't really matter to me how many days my floors were clean. As a matter of fact, my floors were dirty last year, and now that I look back on last year, it doesn't really matter that they were dirty. The world didn't end. I'm going to stop worrying about it. I don't answer to anybody but my own family and so far they're okay with it. Wait, didn't this floor used to be white?)*

3. What can you realistically control in this situation? (Hint: you can never control other people.)

4. What can't you control?

5. How can you let go of what you can't control?

6. Is it time to ask for help? Who can you turn to for help? Is there someone more qualified?

7. Do you ask for help when you need it, or do you feel like you're supposed to figure it all out on your own?

8. What does a superhero/heroine look like? What does a real woman/man look like?

9. You get to define what's important to you—what a superhero looks like. Make a list. How do you want to be described?

10. Who are the people in your life that are important to you? Those are the people you want to please. How do you measure up? Realistically, not on the superhero scale.

Myth #2 I'M ENTITLED TO A HAPPY ENDING

No, actually you're not

"*But that's not fair!*" my four-year-old whines for the gazillionth time because he can't have a little brother like his friend Max. I explain to him that after a pack of melted crayons on the new car seats, smashed fruit snacks ground into the oriental rug, and a bedspread that now looks like a Civil War reenactment, the chance of a new baby is about as likely as the chance that I will sprout wings and fly him to Never Never Land, which was last week's request from my son who has somehow arrived at the conclusion that life should be fair. I did not explain to him that his birth was an unexplained medical phenomenon and, thanks to my age and other medical and monetary factors beyond my control, there will not be another child unless we buy one or steal one, like that lady did on the Uterus Channel. He just wouldn't understand. I'll let Barney explain it to him.

We all grew up hearing our parents tell us that life wasn't fair. You'd think we would learn. But we haven't. If you don't believe me, sit in on a group prayer session sometime. I know, it's not all of them (and definitely not you, I'm sure) but there are some of you out there who are absolutely coming apart over stupid stuff. Yes, I said it—stupid stuff. Fine if your life is in a shambles because you lost your job and your house and you're eating dog food from the trunk of your car. But not okay if you have just spent twenty minutes crying and slobbering to anybody you can find because the new wing of your house is not going to be finished in time for your scrapbooking party. You think I'm exaggerating? I wish.

I spend the majority of my career traveling around the United States, helping people get back up when life knocks them down. And many of you have some serious burdens on your plate. But in the middle of those who are struggling with disease, death, and nightmares I dare not even mention, are those who are feeling just as lost over issues that have to do with fabric samples and who didn't return a casserole dish. You're out there feuding over something she said three years ago, and holding grudges like it was your last piece of bread in a land of famine. I know this is going to sound mean, but the sense of entitlement out there is ridiculous.

You are in America (pretty safe assumption that this book won't become a hit in Yemen) and that does give you certain rights. You have the right to life, liberty, and the pursuit of happiness. You have the right not to be beaten up by your spouse. You have the right to make a better life for yourself. We are equal and we are free, yes. Life is filled with opportunity. But life is not fair. We aren't guaranteed that everything will work out. Nobody can promise you that, and nobody can deliver it, except God—and even He does not promise you that things will go the way you want. The world does not owe you a happily-ever-after. The world does not owe you anything. When we look at it that way, the things we do have seem a lot more precious, now don't they?

Okay, so you're depressed again. I'm sorry. But the first step in conquering the mountain is acknowledging that it's there. Seeing the truth for what it is really will set you free. When you stop feeling like the world has wronged you, you will start feeling blessed for what you do have in a world filled with so much pain. If you walk around expecting life to work out, you will be constantly disappointed. If you are one of those who spends most of his life in the "why me?" lane, it's time to move over in the "why *not* me?" lane. And if your life is going along without any bumps, enjoy it, because no matter how much you try to avoid it, change is coming.

I remember reading an ad over the holidays that said you could get your entire Thanksgiving dinner in a bag, complete with turkey, mashed potatoes, and an overly critical mother-in-law. Get out the paddles for Great Aunt Ethel that such a day would come when holiday food would be poured out of a bag in a house filled with the smells of hot plastic and the sounds of a crackling microwave. I can just see my Granny Jean staring down from that great all-you-can-eat buffet in the sky, curling up her lip and saying, "That is not how Thanksgiving is supposed to be. Now, Peter, you know sweet potatoes go in the gold dish."

When I was growing up, Thanksgiving was about one thing and one thing only: food. Not thankfulness, not pride in how far we've come, but food. Had a run-in with the law? We'll forgive you. Spent last summer naked on a commune chanting "Kumbaya"? We'll pray for you. But bring instant mashed potatoes to a family reunion and you will be shunned for three generations. (I know I already said this earlier, but I liked it so much I put it in there twice. Lower your expectations.)

I remember how relatives came from miles around, descending on Granny Jean's house like ants running towards that last morsel of egg salad left on a deserted picnic table: bringing their newest additions, latest attachments, lingering grudges, philosophies on life, and whatever dish they were known for making, like Aunt Vyrnetta's mashed potato surprise, which taught me that surprise isn't always a good thing. Or Aunt Bitsy's congealed salad wreath filled with fruit cocktail that kept moving a good ten minutes after you set it down, much like Aunt Bitsy herself.

Our stuffing had sage in it, our cornbread had corn in it, our biscuits (yes, biscuits *and* cornbread) were so light and buttery they were known to turn heathens into saints on the spot. And our green beans were so greased up that our lips had a permanent sheen of lard gloss for three days. And no matter how many people were there or how long we stayed, there was always plenty of food.

It was a time when women gathered in the kitchen to whisk and whisper, while children explored nooks and crannies of a house whose dark rooms whispered untold secrets. Men checked out each other's engines (car engines—get your mind out of the gutter) and argued over baseball and politics, while young couples found quiet corners to steal a kiss. There was no television going. There were no faces glued to video games, just the sound of laughter.

I remember the year we were traveling for this annual tradition and the station wagon broke down and we had to trade Granny's warm, fuzzy, holiday buffet for a sticky stool at Ernie's Egg Hut, sharing dinner with three guitar players from Utah and a waitress named Star. We were kids, so it qualified as a new adventure. Who needs a warm fire and soft music when you can have pancakes with whipped topping?

That was the year I learned that things don't always stay the same. And every year as I grow older I watch tiny pieces being chipped away from that warm Thanksgiving painting. No more sage in the stuffing. Fat-free mayonnaise—the horror. Some too busy to come this year. Biscuits from a can. Another empty chair. A sugar-free salad and oyster stew. And sometimes the change is as subtle as the shift in my perspective.

Sometimes it makes me sad and I long for just one of those moments back: just a scent; just to hear that laughter one more time; to feel Granny's warm, biscuit-scented hands wrapped around my face. But, if I'm lucky, I remember that even as I speak I am creating new memories. And just because the memories aren't the same as they once were, they will one day be treasured just as much, whether it's a warm spot by the fireplace or sitting on the seat of a sticky stool in Ernie's Egg Hut, eating pancakes and whipped topping with three guitar players from Utah and a waitress named Star.

Things don't always work out the way we want them to. Not only is that the way it is—it's okay. Because sometimes it's even better. Sometimes it's not. Sometimes it just is what it is.

- Stop thinking that life owes you something

- Be thankful for what life has given you

- Put things in perspective

- Accept life for what it is

- Stop asking, "Why me?"

- Ask, "Why not me?"

Discussion Questions:

1. Make a list of ten things you have to be thankful for. Review this list often and add to it. This list will keep you grounded when you face obstacles. The more you look for blessings in your life, the more you will find.

2. Pick a current or recent stressful situation. (Maybe the washing machine breaks in the middle of a load and it's the third appliance to break down this month and you can't afford to fix any of them because you still haven't finished paying for the work on the car that you now owe more on than it's worth.) Come up with ten things that are worse than that. Now find ten positive things that are a result of these ten situations. This is hard, I know, but just try.

3. Make a list of the things that continue to stress you out.

4. Now look back on last year and make a list of things you regret.

5. Picture yourself at the end of a long-lived life. What will be important to you?

6. Often it is during the tough times that we learn and grow the most. Think of a rough patch you went through and how you were different once you made it through it. (For example, when I was growing up, being the kid they picked on taught me what it was like to have people not like me.

The world didn't end if people didn't like me. I could still find happiness if somebody didn't like me. Now I use those skills as a comedian to deal with hecklers. If I hadn't had the childhood I did, I might never have learned humor to cope.)

•

Myth #3   THE GOOD GUY ALWAYS WINS

Sometimes doing the right thing can get you killed—do it anyway

Can you imagine the look on the audience's face if you get to the end of Cinderella and find out that the charming prince chose the ugly stepsister because she had more money? Or that Cinderella lived happily-ever-after until she caught a flesh-eating disease and even the birds stopped coming around? Or if the fairy godmother had said she could help for six monthly payments of just $19.99? Or what if a robber breaks into a house, trips and breaks his leg, and sues the homeowner for leaving a skateboard on the steps—and wins? Or what if some creepy evil short guy with an ugly mustache convinces thousands of people to help him wipe out an entire race? What about the speaker who gets all the applause and all the fans and all the money—and is completely void of character? What if you're one of the nice guys who does everything right, and she picks the one who is secretly sleeping with all of her friends? What if you read all the parenting books and teach your kids all the rules and feed them all their vegetables, and it's your kid who has pot in his locker? As much as we hate to see it happen, it's true. The good guys don't always win in the end. You can do everything right, and it still doesn't mean you'll win. Which reminds me of a story—but we'll have to travel to Cedar Grove for this one. If you're new, Cedar Grove is the town where my wacky cast of Southern characters lives. They've been quiet for so long. I just couldn't keep them quiet one moment longer.

It has been said that success is what happens when no one is looking, and failure is what happens when everyone is looking. There is the hero who lands a plane on the Hudson, and the silent hero whose name will never be known by more than a few. And then there's the kind of hero that emerges when you announce that you're looking for one. Which is exactly what happened in Cedar Grove, a sleepy little town that falls prey to most of my stories: a tiny, forgotten town about a mile and a hair past nowhere—a place where the simple life is revered, ordinary heroes are appreciated, and the stories aren't fancy, they're just about the people. People who taught me about life and how many ways there are to see it.

The town had become big enough to know what it was now missing, but small enough that you could walk into any establishment, see the stranger in front of you, and within minutes find out you're second cousins. "Does your name tag say 'Barley,' as in the Barleys who used to own the funeral parlor over in Six Forks? Had the kid named Stump, who lost his leg over that whole mishap with the riding mower? Yeah, the one who later married that Jenkins girl, whose older sister ran off and joined the fair to guess your weight? Dude! That's my mamma's second cousin! I think we're related!" It had gotten so bad that they canceled the genealogy workshop over at the community college, feeling that there are some family trees that just shouldn't be climbed.

Cedar Grove was a town that took pride in its families (no matter how tightly interwoven), its lawn ornaments (especially those crafted out of used tires), and its businesses, which while small, took great pride in the hanging of a shingle—which is why the Cedar Grove Chamber of Commerce was thriving, with thirty-five business members and Old Man Peabody, who wasn't technically working anywhere but liked to be included in stuff.

The Chamber staff consisted of a small group of dedicated citizens under the guidance of one Miss Imogene Twitter, whose shrill voice, sour disposition, and eternal expression of disgust at the inadequacy of those around her told you that to Miss Twitter, the Chamber was her life. Miss Twitter was quite convinced she wasn't just part of the Chamber, she *was* the Chamber, and without her they would surely fall into the fiery pits of hell, where it was rumored she spent her vacations. So she would be horrified if I didn't tell you that it was her idea to start the Citizen of the Year Award while making a subtle pitch for herself in the process; for after all, without her, where would the town be? And so an awards committee was formed (which actually consisted of the staff, just with their names in different order) and it was announced that Cedar Grove would pick a citizen who exhibited the same distinguished character and accomplishment as the fine families who had started this town all those years ago—with the exception of the Crawfords, who, it was said, stole horses and didn't return casserole dishes.

It wasn't hard to get the word out—for there is no force in the universe more powerful than gossip fed through an airtight chain of

Baptist women. And pink sponge-rollered heads were seen bobbing all over the town, as word was spread over phone lines, through open kitchen windows, and across white picket fences where people stopped their daily routines to take a life assessment and to envision themselves winning the award, finally enjoying the credit they had so long deserved. For some this would be the closest they would get to fame—to being a star. Everybody look at me—look at me! Then they get followed by mobs of paparazzi and scream, "Stop looking at me! I want privacy!"

There were some who were convinced they had already earned the award and others, who, after careful self-evaluation, found themselves to be lacking and set out to earn the award—some even willing to trade their character to do it. The Chamber started receiving gifts, donations, concert tickets, and even the promise of her next-born child from Bethany Birch, who had nine kids and swore if she got pregnant one more time she was going to teach them to play baseball, form a team, and sell them on eBay.

Anybody with a rich or famous relative played his card—even Skeeter, who claimed he had a cousin who once passed out on the set of Dawson's Creek and still has the jeans with footprints where Katie Holmes walked over him before the cops came (the shoe print lasted on his face for a good three months).

Sherman Oaks, aka Mattress King, the one with the sign in the window that says WE TREAT YOU LIKE FAMILY (which means they ignore you, never return your calls, and are only happy to see you when they need money), decided that his business deserved the award and to prove it, he was going to put all mattresses on sale, which some folks claimed was not a big deal. (Please, when are mattresses not on sale?) But then Sherman was making a delivery and flicked his cigarette out the window of his pickup, and it flew back and landed on the mattress he was delivering and caught on fire, and he had to stop the truck and jump back and pound out the flames, which is how he lost most of his body hair. So he figured he was out—who would give an award to somebody without eyebrows? But the event was so harrowing, added to his new hairless handicap, that he is now convinced he should be a motivational speaker.

The Welcoming Committee over at the Baptist Church decided to better their chances of winning, seeing as how they hadn't really gotten to welcome anybody in years, being as the closest they had to a newcomer was that skinny fellow who was running from the law. And so the women did what they did best—cooked. The Jews have their Star of David, the Catholics have their rosary, and the Baptists have their casserole. Nothing says Citizen of the Year like Aunt Bitsy's congealed salad filled with marshmallows and fruit cocktail and shaped like a cross, of course—the only food that keeps moving a good ten minutes after you set it down, much like Aunt Bitsy herself.

But somewhere between the Bundt cakes and the pink ambrosia salad, they had an altercation that started with the question of whether the green bean casserole should have real mushrooms or canned. It turned into a feud over who got invited to Nora's Scrapbooking for Jesus party. And somehow ended with Beulah May facedown in the mashed potatoes and Ethel Brown commenting on the size of her rear end, and Clara distraught because she just got an email that told her she's dying after putting plastic containers in the microwave—and Myrtle broke the news that she doesn't really have royal relatives in Nigeria who want to send her money. And the casseroles stopped arriving at the Chamber just about the time the first letter arrived in a tiny envelope addressed, "to whom it may concern."

The Cedar Grove Fire Department was "all in a tither" (technically not a phrase, but I'm trying to legitimize it) because what better candidate for citizen of the year than a fireman who risked his life and limb for the safety of his people? But the last time they'd been called anywhere was the time Bert Dinkins swallowed his hearing aid at the Shriners Picnic.

And then Teddy Franklin, who sold orthopedic shoes and coached little league on weekends, had a moment of character weakness and decided to stage his own fire over at Shady Hills Rest Home so he could be on the front page of the paper walking out, covered in soot, carrying a senior citizen and her cat. I know, horrible. But luckily, before he could start the fire, Eulalie Birch had another one of her panic attacks in the next room when she thought the young man who had come in to bring her lunch was that fellow that got all them people to drink the Kool-Aid, and there in her plastic cup, sure enough, was red juice. She started screaming and hyperventilating right before Teddy could start that fire, and he ran in to help and started administering CPR 'cause he'd seen enough episodes of *ER* to consider himself qualified—and if anybody needs an autopsy, thanks to *CSI,* he can now do one in under sixty minutes, and scrape some gunk off the bottom of your shoes in the process and trace it back to some distant tribe in Africa. And you'd better watch out because now he's started watching *Nip/Tuck.*

I'll never forget the time he watched a House marathon and for days made fun of people and walked with a limp. Eulalie turned out to be okay, and now apparently Teddy goes over there on Thursday mornings to sit with her and watch *Judge Judy*. Teddy has been watching it for years—that's how come Eulalie has hired him to write her a will so she can have in writing who is going to get her ceramic cat collection and make sure none of them goes to her half sister Bertie, who had the nerve to wear white at Eulalie's wedding and she still hasn't forgiven her, even considering Eulalie ended up throwing that husband to the curb when she caught him wearing a pair of her favorite heels.

And then another letter arrived at the Chamber.

Granny Jean decided she'd win the award by biking across America eating only beef jerky and wearing a T-shirt that said, MY WILD OATS HAVE TURNED TO SHREDDED WHEAT, but only got as far as Ray Jean's Diner before she got a leg cramp and noticed that they had corned beef on special. So she stopped and ate and came up with her plan to swim the English Channel. Yeah, she's crazy. Not wacky crazy, or silly crazy, but *we're just going to put this nice little white jacket on you* crazy. I heard the other day they caught her chatting on the Internet—with herself. Her husband said he married her for her personality. He just didn't know she had twelve of them. I think her kid should write a children's book and call it, *You have two mommies? That's nothing. I have five.*

Vyrnetta was convinced that her beauty alone made her deserving of the award. She was a woman who was consumed with her personal appearance. There wasn't a body part on that woman hadn't been tucked, sucked, plucked, tweezed, shifted or lifted at one time or another. She had these frighteningly long fingernails that curled at the tips and were painted this color that always matched her lipstick. She had a beauty mole she had designed herself, thick black eyelashes, and wore wigs just about every day of the week. Rumor has it that that woman has a closet just for her own hair. And every one of them wigs has got a kick to it, if you know what I mean, 'cause Aunt Vyrnetta's way of thinking is that when it comes to hair, honey, bigger is better. She wore so much makeup when the street artist at the fair drew her face, he only got halfway through before he ran out of paint. Mamma used to say it was a shame she wasn't proud of the face God give her. Daddy said it was a wonder God even recognized that woman anymore at all. Vyrnetta considered her body a work of art. I do too—mine's just the cheap kind on black velvet they sell at the fair. Yeah, Vyrnetta was fancy all right—not like the two plain letters that arrived at the Chamber that day.

Brandy was sure she would win. She was at least ninety and had been a candy striper over at the medical center so long they claim she once treated Moses for smoke inhalation. Her real name was Berta, but she had started calling herself Brandy somewhere between her third face lift and the series of Botox injections that had left her face in a permanent state of confusion. Anyway, she thought Brandy described how she saw herself: sweet, hot, and dangerous in big doses. And, yes, Brandy was an acquired taste. She was on a quest to find a husband or a sugar daddy, and considered her patients open game, sneaking peaks and pokes whenever given the opportunity. It was not unusual to come out of surgery to see Brandy's blown-up lips in your face, whispering, *"Who's your mamma?"* And then the Chamber got two more letters.

Creepy Cooter could have won the prize based on the fact that he was voted most likely to go postal. Every town's got one: he just kind of lurks around and stares at you under his bangs. Goes to the DMV just to hang out. According to his MySpace site, he is an *athletic forty-year-old looking for a companion, who likes listening to classical music and long walks in the park.* Translated: *Gaunt fifty-year-old looking for someone not carrying mace, who likes listening to classical music from outside your window, and takes long walks in the park to find places to hide the bodies.* And then a handful of letters arrived at the Chamber.

Mrs. Proctor walked a little taller in the secret knowledge that surely she would win the prize. Mrs. Proctor taught third grade and put to death the assumption that all teachers are warm and fuzzy. She was a large woman with big muscles and an incredible cleavage that could store two sodas, a pack of nabs, and an unruly child. She had an unbearable habit of being brutally honest. It was rumored that she ate little children and puppies.

Wade and Bo Junior decided to get in on the action and do something that would make them be remembered for more than sitting on the front porch drinking Old Milwaukee and shooting the empty cans off the dead tree stump. They're pretty much harmless idiots. (Once Bo Junior was filling out this job application and where it asked who to notify in case of emergency, he wrote: a good doctor.) Anyway, the two never had a good idea between them but that sure hasn't stopped them from trying. And as you know, most of the time their Old Milwaukee did the thinking for them. That's how their plan started with a six-pack, grew to include a homemade ramp and a juiced-up scooter, and the famous last words that started with "I can jump that far," and ended with, "Yep, now that's gonna leave a mark."

Harriet, the server over at Bert's Burger Barn, dreamed of winning the award because there was nobody in that town more devoted to her customers. And thanks to her drama classes over at the community college, she had come up with thirty-seven different heartfelt ways to say, "Can I get you anything?" (I hate that when you're waiting on your food in a restaurant and it's taking forever and the waitress keeps coming up and saying, "Your meal isn't ready. Can I get you anything?" Yeah! My food! Imagine if they used that kind of thinking at the ER! "Sir, I know you're coding and we're short on help because the surgeon's on break and we're out of paddles but (pause) can I get you anything?")

And then there was Mildred's cousin Nester who used to be an exotic dancer and chose his stage name, "Rambo," to match the scar on his face that he said he got in a fight but actually came from the time he tried to twirl a baton perched on a lawn chair. Anyway, he went to get his name tattooed on his arm and had just gotten some dental work done and was still woozy, and the artist didn't hear him correctly with him slurring his words, and Nester woke to find that instead of "Rambo," "Rainbow" had been tattooed on his arm—which sent his career in a whole other direction. He's started his own drama club and they're about to premier their new show: *Deliverance, the Musical*.

What wasn't normal was the amount of letters coming in to the Chamber. Or the fact that they were all about the same person.

And then there was Utility Bench. (I know, weird name: her dad was in construction and had really wanted a boy.) She was a real hero because she had offered up her uterus to her sister's cousin, who couldn't have children. And that's a citizen right there—even if she did charge her so she could pay for a new wing on her trailer. But it was still a good deed.

What most of these people didn't know was that the hero had already been chosen. As it turns out, they didn't have to find him—the winner found them, in the pages of letter after letter. Letters written by different hands, with different stories, but letters that all told the story of a shy little man who swept floors and changed lives. A shy man with a stutter who swept the floors over at Ray Jean's Diner every morning and every afternoon. His name was Stevie. "Just Stevie," he called himself, because he had grown up hearing people who pointed in his direction ask, "Who is he?" and being told, "Oh, that's just Stevie." Just Stevie wore a baseball cap, didn't look you directly in the eye, and never missed a day of work, no matter what.

And if you were to walk into Ray Jean's diner and see him, you would probably not consider him the most likely choice for Citizen of the Year, or even in the running. You would have had to have been there on the day Stevie went with Will to his first dentist appointment and sat there and held his hand. You would have had to have been there when Stevie watered Shirley's roses when she left to go take care of her daughter. Or when Stevie sat with the little Jenkins boy while he colored and waited for his mother, who often forgot to pick him up. When he sat with Perry after he lost his son, long after everyone else had gone. When Stevie danced with Brandy on Valentine's Day because he knew she always got sad that time of year. When Homeless Pete forgot his lunch money again, and Stevie handed him the five dollars he had been saving for the movies. When nobody would play the part of the sheep in the church pageant—Stevie did it. When they needed somebody to stand outside and hold the flag at football games—Stevie volunteered. When Mrs. Proctor's cat Buttons died, it was Stevie who helped her bury him.

And as we watched Stevie shuffle up to receive his award without meeting our eyes, we were reminded that heroes come in all shapes and sizes. There are some who land a plane on the Hudson, and others whose names will never be known by more than a few. Stevie reminded us of the tremendous power we have to make a difference.

I believe that life gives you moments—opportunities—that were put in your path for a reason: moments when you are uniquely qualified to play your card. It can be as simple as a word spoken when someone really needed to hear it. Moments when you alone have tremendous power to make a difference. Stevie reminded us that it isn't about what moment you're given—it's whether you take it. What about you? Will you be that hero that comes along when nobody is looking?

Just another lesson taught to me by those wacky characters in that tiny forgotten town about a mile and a hair past nowhere, where the simple life is revered, ordinary heroes are appreciated, and the stories aren't fancy, they're just about the people. People who taught me about life, and all the many ways to see it.

Isn't that a great story? I wish it really ended that way, but it didn't. Oh, Stevie should have won the award, but he didn't. Thurm Decker won the award because he knew the right people. And the next year it went to somebody who had paid for the new wing at the hospital. Stevie died that year, and at his funeral he was surrounded by people who really loved him, whose lives had been touched by that shy little man who swept floors at Ray Jean's Diner. He never got a certificate or his picture in the paper. But I have a feeling that long after the paint has peeled on the Town Hall, people won't remember who won all those awards, but they'll still be talking about Stevie.

- Doing the right thing doesn't mean you'll always come out on top. Do the right thing anyway.
- The number of cheering fans is never an indication of a man's character. It's what you do when nobody is looking that counts.

Discussion Question:

If I'm going to do everything right and still not win, why try?

Myth #4   POOR LITTLE HELPLESS PRINCESS

You are not a victim

What if Cinderella's fairy godmother had never come along? Would she have pined away forever? Would she have been eighty years old, scrubbing floors, and singing to the squirrels about her true love who will be here any minute? So many of our fairy-tale princesses are waiting helplessly for someone or something to come and save them. I remember waiting for my charming prince. When I was nineteen, I wanted him to be handsome, rugged, and wealthy. When I was twenty, I was willing to go for nice and employed. When I was thirty, I didn't care who he was, as long as he had a pulse and could dress himself. I remember thinking that my life wouldn't start until I got married, or until the perfect job came along, or until I reached the ideal size. We're always waiting for something that we're sure will make us complete, when the answer is to learn how to be complete just as we are—to realize that no matter where we are in life, we are not a victim of our circumstances. I learned that from the Hot Flashes.

It wasn't too long ago when I found myself sitting in the airport, convinced that my life was as good as over: broke, fifty pounds over my goal weight (realizing it was too late for me to become an actress, having just found a hair on my chin), and surrounded by seven blue-haired women in red hats and purple T-shirts that read: HOT FLASHES HIT HAWAII. STAND TOO CLOSE AND YOU'LL GET BURNED. IF YOU CAN READ THIS T-SHIRT WITHOUT YOUR GLASSES, YOU DON'T QUALIFY FOR MEMBERSHIP. So much for blending in. I tried to remember how to make a noose.

Agnes and Betty Lou were already arguing about who was going to get the bed by the bathroom, Clara had already knitted four scarves and was deep into a sweater, and Doreen was putting the stamp on her third "wish you were here" postcard. Ermadetta was writing out an itinerary that centered around her daily nap. Fay was sleeping and snoring loudly as she clutched her I LOVE HAWAII bag. And Gertrude (my aunt Trudy) was pouring over bridesmaids' dresses for the wedding she was planning upon her return, to the fiancé she was planning to find in Hawaii. I was to be her maid of honor, she announced, showing me a pink chiffon dress that looked like something churned out of the cotton candy machine at the county fair, only bigger. I wondered if the psych ward was taking new patients, because I was going to need a room by the end of this week. I made a mental note to buy some cardigans.

We had not even left the ground and I was already regretting my promise to chaperone Aunt Trudy and her red-hat ladies to Hawaii, even though I had never been to Hawaii and my mother was paying me to accompany Aunt Trudy to make sure she didn't get married, and since she couldn't be trusted to travel on her own ever since that year she set out for the grocery store and ended up in a topless bar on the other side of town. We did not know Trudy knew how to dance around a pole. She said she would teach me sometime, that it was a skill every woman should have, was great for your calves, and she had left a message for the dean at the college to see if he wanted her to teach a course. I reminded myself never to run for public office, and drooled at the idea of how many medications I now had at my disposal if I decided to take myself out. And it was no longer a matter of *if*, but merely a question of *when*.

We hit Hawaii with a force that could only be described as that of tsunami strength. Everywhere we went, you could hear those ladies from down the block. Their noisy chatter and chicken-like cackling announced the arrival of the massed red-and-purple pack as they marched determinedly in their special Hawaiian-themed orthopedic shoes, their red hats bobbing furiously and matching them step for step. I was trying to decide between an open casket or having my ashes scattered, favoring the latter because while I didn't like the idea of being burned, I would look thinner that way.

They faced each moment in Hawaii as a new adventure, and each day brought a story I knew would stick with me forever—and come to haunt me later in the form of late-night sweats. For the sake of time, I will just give you the highlights. Oh, where should we start? How about Agnes catching her head on fire? Agnes caught her head on fire when she stood too close to the bonfire at the Hawaiian luau. She was wearing her new artificial synthetic silver wig, shaped like a cone and adorned with plastic pink flowers, and apparently did not see the tag on it that said HIGHLY FLAMMABLE. She got so carried away when it was her turn at karaoke to sing "Moon over Miami," that she didn't notice how close she was to the flames and when she bent over backwards at the end of the song for dramatic effect, her synthetic wig got close enough to catch a spark, which quickly caused her precious hair to go up in flames. Luckily, we all knew to stop, drop, and roll her, which put the fire out, ruined the wig, but, in a way, achieved the dramatic effect she had been seeking all along. You should have seen that pantyhose-stocking-looking thing she had on under that wig—I guess to hold her hair in place. She was a fright. Looked like she was about to rob us, and a couple of people actually hit the deck. I was so embarrassed that I almost threw myself in the fire, but I don't like to be hot.

Betty Lou had purchased a strapless sarong that was technically a size too small, hence the additional purchase of a girdle that was guaranteed to hold up under the most extreme pressure. I'm not sure that Girdle Tester #29 could have foreseen the pressure that particular girdle was going to be asked to withstand from Betty Lou, who was quite a sizeable woman, or from the wave that was destined to crash into her when she waded too far out in the water so she could fit into the lens of Doreen's camera for the photo that was going to go on that scrapbook page titled, "Hot Flashes Hit the Beach." It's hard to say whether blame should be placed on the wave or on Betty's third trip to the late-night chocolate buffet at the hotel, but it was enough pressure to completely disrobe Betty's upper torso in a matter of seconds—girdle and all. That girdle just couldn't hold up under pressure, and neither could Betty Lou.

We stared in disbelief at the sight of her screaming and jumping up and down (which didn't help her case) and trying to cover what could not humanly be covered. Three life guards dove in to save her, which was good because if one had tried to go put his arms around her, I'm afraid he would have just disappeared. She was scared, but not hurt, and swore she was writing a letter to those sarong people to tell them their product had scarred her for life. Only I'm not sure she was as scarred as the ones on the beach who had witnessed the whole endeavor, including the Asian couple taking pictures like this was some kind of *National Geographic* moment. I made a mental note that drowning myself might not be the best way to go. And then we lost Clara.

Clara was probably the sweetest and most agreeable person in the group—not due to good intentions, but due to the fact that she had been pretty close to stone-cold deaf since 1982. And rather than get a hearing aid, she just nodded and smiled at everything you said. Which is why people liked her, because she was so darn agreeable. But this also caused her to get overly inebriated at dinner, because whenever the waiter stopped and asked if she'd like a refill on her drink, she would just smile and nod, and say the only Hawaiian phrase she had learned, which didn't stand for "what a beautiful view" like she thought it did, but rather, "May I have another gin and tonic?" Who can tell with all those vowels?

So, in this state, she was often apt to wander off after dinner, which is how she headed to the restroom and ended up on the wrong tour bus. And instead of sitting with a group of sweet blue-haired ladies holding cardigans and cameras, found herself on a bus full of overly made-up cross-dressers who might have had large Adam's apples, but could certainly accessorize. And is how she found her long-lost cousin Fred (now called Frieda), who had supposedly run off with his secretary ten years ago. Turns out he'd never had an affair with the secretary—only thing she ever did for him was teach him how to walk in high heels. When we went to rescue Clara, one of them told me I'd look better as a blonde. I made a note to purchase a bottle of hair dye as soon as I got home. And drink it.

Doreen, bless her heart, was a flighty woman who had stopped thinking once and never got started back up. She fell asleep in the sun without any sunscreen and turned a gruesome shade of red, except for around her eyes where she had worn oversized sunglasses. She looked like a burn victim. She lost her teeth in a poker match and dropped an orthopedic shoe in a volcano. It took three men to keep her from jumping in after it—that was the last shoe made like that. We forgave her; after all, she just wasn't in her right mind after all that chocolate at the sugar factory where you could sample the chocolates, and Doreen then disappeared for hours—worried us sick—until finally she appeared with a black ring around her mouth claiming she had not been eating chocolate, like her diet forbid, but was in fact fighting with a homeless woman out back who was wearing her orthopedic shoes. I'm sure she lied about the chocolate.

Ermadetta wore her RED HATS FOR JESUS ball cap and held daily spiritual reenactments on the beach at sunrise, which is probably the first-ever reenactment where the Jesus wore a red hat and a T-Shirt that said: DON'T LET THIS GRAY HAIR FOOL YOU. THERE MAY BE SNOW ON THE ROOF BUT THERE'S FIRE IN THE KITCHEN. Her enactments didn't go over so well with the heathens and those of the homeless persuasion who were forced to act like disciples.

Fay was intent on finding a mug that said I LOVE HAWAII to go with her I LOVE MYRTLE BEACH and I LOVE DOLLYWOOD mugs, and made us sift through two hundred key chains to find just the right one for her granddaughter Ruth. Then we had to comb the beaches looking for famous people, and she got mad when she couldn't find Jennifer Anniston or Brad Pitt, or that big-lipped hussy woman he had taken up with and broken poor Jennifer's heart. And she was going to find him and give him a piece of her mind. But she got distracted when she swore she saw Conway Twitty, and she chased that poor man for three blocks trying to get his autograph, despite the fact that it was quite obvious he was using his cell phone to call the police. She finally got distracted thinking she saw Jerry Springer, who really turned out to be Jerry Springer, and I'll be darned if Fay didn't have a spot on his show that next week. I wouldn't be able to see it. I'd be dead by then.

My Aunt Trudy never let up on her quest to find a husband and, to our surprise, found one on the very first day—a sweet mild-mannered gentleman ten years her junior who I don't think in all honesty even knew they were dating. We're afraid Trudy was somewhat misled by his intentions and mistook his attentive nature for courtship, when actually he was the steward coming by every day to clean her room. But you know Trudy—bullheaded—and she spent three hours making him sample the cakes for the wedding. I actually considered putting off my suicide until after the wedding.

When we left, there was more than one sigh of relief—from flight attendants, wait staff, bus drivers, policemen, homeless people, and the guy who tried to paint graffiti on the overpass (don't ask). Once we were gone, there were only pieces left as evidence that we had been there at all: Betty Lou's girdle stuffed into a lounge chair; pieces of Agnes's hair blowing in the wind; new red-and-purple knitted scarves around the necks of cross-dressers; and the faint scent of chicken-like chatter and an occasional flashback of a red hat bobbing determinedly. The things you could see and those you couldn't; the tiny doses of hope to those who needed to see it. The sound of laughter from those who'd forgotten how. The encouragement to those who so desperately needed something to hang on to: the encouragement that you are never too old, too poor, too weak, or too broken-hearted to have fun in life.

Those quirky women in their red hats—who I was so sure would be the last nail in my coffin—were actually what saved me. A bunch of old women who taught me that life is far from over: women who brought silliness back into my life and who reminded me that we are all in this together. Life brings hardship and pain, but we don't have to go through it alone or weary or sad. There are those we can grab on to—those who share a bond of affection and common experiences. We can join our red-gloved hands together and march determinedly into wherever life takes us next.

The Red Hats have grown beyond what was ever imagined, and will continue to grow. Why? Because somewhere out there is always another woman who is lonely, with a red hat collecting dust in her closet, waiting for someone to come with outstretched hand and remind her that life is far from over—that the fun is just beginning. I gave Mom her money back. I couldn't take money for that. Not when they gave me the gift. A gift I could never repay.

As it turns out, Trudy is getting married next month to a sweet fellow she met on the plane-ride home who loves her just the way she is. They're getting married in Vegas. The Hot Flashes are all invited. All I've got to say is: Look out, Vegas, because the Hot Flashes are coming, and nobody's safe, especially not Wayne Newton and Elvis.

- It's never too late to rewrite your script

- You are not a victim

- Life is what you choose to make of it

- Get rid of the excuses and start changing your life

- Take the words "I can't" out of your vocabulary and replace them with "why not?"

Discussion Questions:

1. Is there something that you have always dreamed of doing? Why not do it before it's too late?

2. When you retire, what will you want to do more than anything else? Why not do it now? Have you always wanted to write, paint, or take a cooking class? Do it.

3. Analyze your excuses for not doing what will bring you joy. Is it because you think you're too old? Are you really? Is it because you don't have time? Make time. Is it because you're scared? Jump anyway.

Myth #5   PRINCESSES NEED A COLON CLEANSE

Redefining Beauty

Just once, I'd like to see a fairy tale starring a princess with a bad perm and a harelip, or a superhero with a gut and a comb-over. I tried wearing the ball gown and the ballet slippers and a strand of pearls, and it just didn't work for double-coupon day over at Food Mart. I'd like to open a magazine and see a model that actually eats three times a day. That's why she looks so miserable—she's hungry.

And I would like to take a moment to thank TiredOfYourWeight@Who'sTheNextIdiot.com for the email you just sent reminding me that I'm overweight. Thanks. I had forgotten until you sent that sweet little message in my inbox to remind me how fat I am. How did you find me? Were you there when I used emergency money to buy Girl Scout cookies? When I dove between the sofa cushions because I thought I saw a French fry? When I ran past you in my bathing suit at the pool and took out three toddlers? How do you people know that I want to lose weight, need money transferred from

Nigerian royalty, and have been looking everywhere for a fake Rolodex? Baffling.

So, Mister TiredOfYourWeight, I appreciate that you took time in the middle of the night to send me this urgent email to share your weight-loss secret that is sure to revolutionize the world, and to give me the opportunity to buy into it before anyone else. I am flattered that you spend so much time and energy caring about strangers. I wish you would spend the same amount of time learning to spell and removing the strands of gibberish in your heartfelt message which, until I speak in tongues, I am unable to translate. I'm sure you mean well, but I don't need the revolutionary answer to instant weight loss. You see, I already know the answer—and have known it for years. In fact, it really hasn't been much of a secret since fourth-grade biology: Eat less than you have been, exercise more than you have been, and you will lose weight. Shocking, I know. Knowing what to do isn't my problem—doing it is.

You see, I would rather drink lumpy shakes made out of goat's urine, strap thirty pounds of spandex to my body, and spend thousands of dollars on hairdos, clothes, and accessories guaranteed to make me look a size smaller. I would rather have my colon flushed and take diet pills that cause hair loss, fainting spells, and the unavoidable explosive diarrhea. It may be embarrassing, but by golly I'll be skinny. But don't make me eat vegetables—that's just gross. I want those programs where you actually pay more to eat less. I would rather spend hours reading manuals from experts claiming it's not the quantity but the combinations of foods—just don't mix the brown Snickers with the tan French fries and you're fine.

I want to sit around perplexed, saying, "But I don't eat *that much,*" and convince myself that I must have some rare thyroid condition and that everybody's order contains the word *Supersize.* I want to buy exercise tapes that I'm too lazy to open and fancy treadmills to hold my plants, rather than park at the back of the parking lot and take the stairs. I am not interested in the kind of exercise where I am involved. I don't even want to get up to change the TV. I once watched a twenty-four-hour Henry Winkler marathon because I couldn't find the remote. I would rather sit around with a group of other overweight people and have them tell me size doesn't matter, while we look at skinny people in disgust and hope they're miserable.

So I do know the secret to weight loss, *Mr. TiredOfYourWeight.* Perhaps if you could come up with a revolutionary way to do the things we don't want to do—now that I would read. So thanks, but no thanks. I would, however, be interested in a way to earn a million in a week without ever having to get dressed or leave my house. Do you have a cousin who does that?

As you can see, I have issues with the way society dictates what beautiful is. And yet I still fall into that trap over and over. Like with my eyebrows. Did I tell you that one? Settle in, because you have just got to hear about this.

"That's it. I've had it," I dramatically announced to my husband as we sat in bed reading. He rolled his eyes, no doubt wondering if this was going to be a repeat of last night's tirade when I'd had enough of telemarketers. Or the night before when I'd had enough of toys that required a mechanic's degree to get them opened. "These glasses have been crooked for three years," I said with the same shocked look I had when I realized not everybody stuffs their pet and puts it by the front door.

"I told you to get them adjusted. Takes five minutes," he murmured, without looking up from his magazine.

That has always been one my weaknesses—those little five-minute tasks, like rotating the tires, checking the fire alarm batteries, and finding out why I can't hear out of my left ear on Saturdays. But this time I decided to follow through. I pulled into the vision place across the street, marched up to the counter and said, "These glasses are really crooked. I need them adjusted." The clerk stared at the mangled glasses that looked like they'd just spent a Friday night wedged in the back seat of Lindsey Lohan's limo while she whispers, "I'm not drunk. I'm just stressed." The clerk left with my glasses, returned two seconds later, and I was on my way. They felt great. Until I got home to a mirror and saw that they were still crooked.

"OH......MY......GOSH!" I yelled, as my husband came running into the bedroom, still dripping from his unfinished shower.

"What? What is it?" he yells in alarm.

"They're STILL crooked!" I shout.

So I had to go back the next day. Now I'm mad. One time was fine, but two trips—this was insane. I held an imaginary conversation in my head with the incompetent clerk who was obviously out to get me and probably made it her life's mission to send people into the world with crooked vision. "They're still crooked," I said through gritted teeth, with a smile and an expression that said, "I'm on to you, little missy. Bringing me out here twice. You must not know who I am and what my time is worth. I'm a storyteller. I speak for a living. All it'll take is one word and I can bring you down." Yes, I have a look that says all that. Just ask the dry cleaner.

She sighed, smiled back, and gave me a look that said, "If I didn't need this job I'd smack you—whoever you think you are—and it can't be 'all that,' considering I saw your jacket on the clearance table at the Thrifty Mart." She sauntered off to adjust my glasses. "Let's make sure they fit, okay?" she said. "Before you leave." She placed the glasses on and they felt great. We looked in the mirror. Still crooked.

"See? I'm not crazy!" I squealed, while she got this expression that said she begged to differ.

"Yep. They're crooked," she answered.

"Well, can you fix it?" I said in my slow-motion sarcastic voice, drawing each word out like she'd been suddenly struck deaf.

"The glasses are straight," she said pointedly. "I'm afraid it's you that's crooked." I swear she smirked.

"What?" I squeaked. I thought I had already conjured up every disorder that could possibly exist, and now come to find that I might have a crooked face? Wait till I tell Mom. Did I get it from her? Do I come from a long line of crooked-headed women and I'm just the first to find out about it? Was that why they were all staring at me at the license renewal place? Get me to the Internet. I've got to see if there are others who've been struck by this phenomenon. Perhaps there is a support group. "Well, can't you just make the glasses crooked?" I asked, giving her the same look I gave the cashier who thought Obama was a terrorist.

"Can't bend them anymore or they'll break." She actually looked happy to be telling me this.

"This is the strangest thing I've ever seen! Do you get other people in here like this?" I asked. I am oddly comforted by the misfortune of others.

"Oh, yeah, all the time. Sometimes people have one ear higher than the other, or maybe it's the eyebrows. Yeah, sometimes they have one eyebrow higher than the other. Maybe that's your problem." She stared intently at my face. "Yeah, that's it. Look! You've got one eyebrow higher than the other."

And that's when the problem slowly shifted into focus. My cheeks reddened and I rushed out of the store before she could figure out that my uneven eyebrows were not blamed on nature, but on my unsteady hand as I groggily drew them on every morning. I sat in the car and stared at what was now so obvious. I had been drawing my eyebrows on crooked. Sure enough, one eyebrow was a good quarter inch higher than the other. I had been walking around for years looking like a circus freak. I had been walking around with a mixed expression of confusion and surprise on my face. No wonder they stared at me. No wonder the other mothers shielded their kids when I came around. No wonder those door-to-door church people kept coming back. How could this have happened to me? Even more, how could my husband not have noticed? This was all his fault. I was waiting for him when he got home from work—sitting in the dark holding an empty glass. "How could you?" I whispered to this man I no longer knew.

"What?" he answered without stopping as he marched into the kitchen for a drink, totally ruining my dramatic effect.

"How could you not tell me?"

"Good grief," he said. "Not this autism thing again. I told you, you're not autistic. Just because you get stressed when your routine is broken doesn't mean anything. A little nuts. A little OCD, but not autistic."

"Not that," I answered. "My eyebrows. How could you not tell me my eyebrows were crooked? After all these years?"

"Who told you that?" he asked, coming in for a closer look.

"The girl at the vision place told me. They're crooked."

"Weird," he said. He opened the paper and began to read.

"That's all you can say?"

"What do you want me to say?"

"Nothing. I just want you to notice me every once in a while. To notice when one eyebrow is higher than the other. All it took was one look—one tiny look. And you couldn't even do that. All you had to say was that my eyebrow was crooked and I could have erased it and started over and we wouldn't be having this conversation and the neighbors wouldn't think I'm a freak."

"The neighbors already thought you were a freak long before that. You were the one who got locked out of the house in your stilettos and curlers. You were the one who didn't know the punch at the Jenkins' birthday party was spiked and crawled into the dog's bed and fell asleep. And what do you mean you'll erase it and start over?" I had finally gotten his attention.

"My eyebrow. If I'd known it was crooked I would have erased it and drawn it lower." I showed him what I meant by rubbing one eyebrow furiously until there was nothing left but a couple of invisible hairs. He actually backed away from me.

"Are you telling me you draw your eyebrows on? With one of those pencil things? Like my Great Aunt Ethel, who uses a cigarette holder and carries her dog in her purse?"

"Yes," I answered, suddenly wondering if this fell into that category of things a man wouldn't understand, kind of like how I can actually see better once I have my eyeliner on, or how it is worth it to wear those suck-me-in panties and look a size smaller even if it does squash my ovaries. "Yes, I draw my eyebrows on." I said it like every woman did it. As if he was the one who was nuts. It didn't work. I could hear him laughing all the way from the garage, where I had marched in anger after grabbing my keys and saying only that I was "going out"—as if to insinuate that he should be worried—when really I was going out to drown my sorrows in a double-fudge waffle cone with sprinkles, which always makes me feel better. I needed to get out. I just wish I had remembered that I was now missing one eyebrow.

So you see, I am no stranger to falling into this trap. We want to look nice. We want to be attractive, but where does it stop? At what point do we stop and say, "Okay, teeth shouldn't be so white that they glow in the dark, my skin doesn't need to be the color of beef jerky, and if I get one more lip injection they're going to call social services." I'm not really sure, but I think we need to stop at the point where our entire sense of self-worth and happiness is wrapped up in our outward appearance. When we find that we're dressing like our kids—and even our kids shouldn't be dressing that way—we're in trouble. When our kindergartner is gyrating hips and trying to make cleavage—and he's a boy—we're in trouble. When everything she looks at, watches, and sings to, screams to her that she needs to be skinny and work on her seduction skills. When you get an email that suggests you could benefit from a butt blast—and you actually consider it. True peace doesn't come with an applicator. Pretty people seem happy, but they're really trying desperately to stay prettier than everybody else, because if they lose that, then they're nothing—or so they think. Quit trying to be a princess—embrace being a frog every once in a while. Life would sure be a lot easier. I've got to go now; I heard there's a new mascara out that will triple my lashes. This is what I have been waiting for.

- Release the unrealistic expectations of how you should look

- Happiness does not come when you are prettier than the others

- Don't let the world define beauty for you

- Teach your children not to be controlled by their outward appearance

Discussion Questions:

- Listen to some of the music that your children are listening to and make a list of what it is telling them.

- Now turn on the videos and make a list of the values that are being promoted. I think you will be appalled.

- Are you obsessing about your body? Do you avoid mirrors? Do you think to yourself that nobody here likes you because you are ugly?

- Think of your closest friends—the people you like most in the world. Why do you like them? Do you like any of them because of how they look?

- What does society tell us beauty looks like? Do you agree? What do you think beauty should look like? Do you know any role models today who uphold these values? Why not make sure your children have the right models?

- What do your children hear you say about your body—or about other people's bodies? Do you stand around commenting on the way others look? Do you even think it?

Myth #6   WAIT FOR THE WIZARD

Don't spend weeks on something you could have fixed in a day

Sometimes there's an easier way to solve the problem than waiting on the wizard to fix it, dodging bullets and screeching monkeys, or riding through the night on a magic carpet. Sometimes we spend more time worrying about what to do than the time it would have taken to fix it. I learned that with the raccoons. Yes, I said raccoons.

I don't mind raccoons that peek at me from the bushes. I don't mind running across an occasional petrified raccoon on the side of the road. I will not lie: they are not on my list of favorite animals, and if they were ever in danger of becoming extinct, I can't say I would quit my job and join the cause. Safe to say that raccoons and I have a mutual understanding. They don't come near me and I don't run them over in my car. That mutual respect was broken, however, when Roger Raccoon took up residence in my attic.

I was young, single, and renting a house with three other girls. My room was the attic-turned-bedroom upstairs. I was at that vulnerable age where up until then my knowledge of fear had been limited to campy horror movies and running out of beer money. I had no glimpse of the fears that I would face as an adult: taxes, gravity, and the inability to hold my bladder when I sneeze. I was encapsulated in this cocoon of ignorance until Roger Raccoon and his family moved into the crawl space adjacent to my attic bedroom. I know it was a family because they fought constantly and I could hear them washing dishes over the faint tune of *Little House* reruns.

There was no loud music to indicate a collegiate atmosphere. Had they been frat brothers, I would have seen the empty cans and pizza boxes. Looking back, I now know the source of the loud thump I heard in the attic that time that I was too chicken to check into it. I figured if it was a dead body it wouldn't start stinking until next semester and I'd be gone. But, no, it was merely Roger moving the furniture. I wasn't sure what the landlord had stored in that attic, but I swore I could hear the whoosh of an exercise bike during Leno.

It started with scratching. By "it" I mean the nightly noises that turned my warm, cozy den into a chamber of terror. Little tiny scratches—I'm thinking hangman on the wall, or perhaps a lively game of charades. I called the landlord, who, unlike the real Lord, did not take my call. He obviously did not appreciate the gravity of the situation—that or he knew that his contract covered him should I have a heart attack on the premises.

I soon learned that Roger and his family kept different hours than I did. When I turned off the light, they came to life. So I tried sleeping with the light on, but as soon as my head hit the pillow they would start up again. So I tried sleeping sitting up, like my Great Aunt Esther in the wingback on Thanksgiving. I give her credit; that's harder than it looks.

I looked on the Internet and found forty-seven thousand articles on how to get rid of a raccoon peacefully. For the record, none of them worked: not even tribal chanting, ostrich mating calls, and Conway Twitty's Greatest Hits. I tried telling them about Amway. I even loaned them money, because you never see people after you loan them money. I tried the one thing guaranteed to make most people run in the other direction: I asked them how they felt about Jesus. They slipped a tract under my door and a black velvet airbrushed painting of a raccoon with his arms outstretched, wearing sandals and a robe.

My friends thought it was funny. *Tell the story, tell the story,* they'd beg at parties. I got lots of laughs. Then the raccoons had a family reunion and invited their inbred cousins, the squirrels, who had so much fun they decided to move in and freeload and let their kids run through the walls at night screaming. Now it wasn't so funny. It had been months and I'd had enough.

I called the police. For future reference, the police aren't interested in that raccoon unless he's driving drunk. I called 911. They asked me to put my mother on the phone. I called pest control, who said they aren't allowed to kill them, but would be happy to come and take them to a sunny place and set them free (I suggested the police department). They said they would be there three weeks from Tuesday, while I wondered if I would still be alive by then, as I pictured my petrified body propped up in Roger's front doorway holding umbrellas and windbreakers.

I was wild-eyed and three steps to crazy by the time the pest-control guy showed up, and I kissed him right on the lips, tobacco and all. He set two traps with a peanut butter sandwich and in five minutes Roger and his family had taken the bait. I know this, because pest-control guy picked up his cell, dialed, and in his best John Wayne voice said, "Herb, get over here quick. We done caught us a coon."

I have to admit that I was a little excited to meet Roger, now that I knew he was moving. I couldn't wait to pucker up and blow tiny kisses at his cute, little, fuzzy raccoon body. Roger turned out to be the size of a small dog. When pest-control guy brought him down hissing and spitting and biting the rungs of the cage, well, let's just say I knew I was off his Christmas party list. The second cage brought the wife and children, who bore a striking resemblance to Roger. My neighbors had all gathered around the front porch to watch the festivities and ask me questions. I felt like one of those people being interviewed after the neighbor gets arrested for serial killing. "He was such a nice quiet man. Never gave us a minute's trouble."

Roger is gone. I can only hope to a place where he can still paint and homeschool the children. The attic space never got new renters while I was there—apparently, word got out about what happened to Roger and his family, and the raccoons put us on some sort of neighborhood profiling list.

But you know what's weird? Since then I've managed to kill (not by my own hand—all natural deaths) three goldfish, four cats, a gerbil, a dog, and a chipmunk who never realized he was my pet. But somehow in the grand irony of things I just know that Roger still runs free. I think he's even got his own reality TV show.

I tell you all of this for a reason. Because it's funny. But really, there's actually a point. I'm ashamed to admit how long I waited before I did anything. How long I allowed myself to be miserable. How long I spent doing nothing but talking about it to anyone who would listen. I was waiting for the wizard to come and fix it. I was waiting for it to go away. Mistake. I stressed for weeks and it took about five minutes to catch him. Sometimes you've just got to quit complaining and wondering who can fix it—and just do it already.

- Don't waste time worrying about the problem
- Quit expecting other people to solve it for you

Discussion question:

Is there something you've been worrying about that you could have fixed by now?

Myth #7   WOLF AND BUNNY ARE FRIENDS

Sometimes you have to love your neighbor from a distance

Isn't it sweet how in fairy tales the bears and the rabbits link arms and sing together? Yeah, I guess the fairy tale wouldn't go over well with the kids if the friendly bear came out and tore the sweet little rabbit apart limb by limb. The animals all love each other and get along swimmingly while they dance and sing show tunes. And the pirates—aren't they just cool? That's what all the boys want to be right now—pirates. Apparently, Barney hasn't done the rape-and-pillage episode. Fairy tales tell us that everybody gets along. Well, they've never met my family. Allow me a moment to share with you a recollection from my childhood.

I was two, and according to my bib, a PRECIOUS LITTLE GIFT FROM HEAVEN, which apparently was under evaluation after that seven-hour car ride where I threw three temper tantrums, stuck a jelly bean up my nose, choked on a plastic frog, and timed each poopy to occur after we passed the rest stop.

We were at the beach, judging by the smell of battered fish and overabundance of joggers wearing thongs. It was another family reunion with Mommy's family—who, according to Daddy, doesn't have a brain cell or a complete set of teeth between them—crammed into what was advertised as a "quaint waterfront cottage," which turned out to be a tiny, bug-infested trailer overlooking a sewage drain. That explains why Uncle Buford had some rental money left over for lottery tickets.

I was a good sport for the first several hours of sand-filled diapers, gritty bologna sandwiches, pinches on the cheek, and requests to hear my off-key rendition of "Twinkle, Twinkle, Little Star." I held it together when Raynelle walked out in her new swimsuit (I've had band aids bigger) and Granny Jean told her she was going to hell. Granny is convinced that half of us are going to hell and the half who aren't should be. I kept my cool when I had to sit with Uncle Buford, who on a good day thinks the year is 1956 and he's a runner for the mob. And I did not let my temper slip when Aunt Edna started slurring her words and crying over her cat Bootsy, who died when she was twelve.

But I was only two, for gosh sakes; I had my limits. And by the time the sun set on our rusty trailer, my patience had worn thin. It was time for some payback. I chose bedtime as the perfect opportunity. Bedtimes are always a good opportunity. I must admit that I had mastered the art of bedtime stall tactics. So after six books, two kisses, four glasses of water, and a bedtime prayer that would have made Moses proud, I had my Mommy just where I wanted her—with her eyes glazed over and her mouth gone slack. It was time to bump things up a notch. I picked that moment to call out for my Yucky-Yucky, who I knew full well had been left behind at our house, sleeping soundly in the guest-room commode where I left it.

I know it's an odd name for my most beloved object of affection. But Yucky-Yucky was not your average childhood treasure. Not one of those cute plush animals delivered to me at birth by a line of blue-haired well-wishers from the local Baptist Church, but an old plastic naked doll with chopped-up hair, a face covered with red Magic Marker, and a missing pinky, delivered straight out of the mouth of the dog next door—and not too willingly, might I add. "NO, NO!" Mommy kept shrieking. "That's the dog's toy. It's yucky, baby. It's yucky, yucky." Hence the name.

I made it clear that I wanted Yucky-Yucky and that I would do anything, including holding my breath, to get it. It was at that particular moment that all eyes turned on me, and pandemonium ensued as the entire cast of wacky Southern characters descended on me like the seagulls on the Cheetos we had tossed out on the beach.

I screamed. I kicked. I held my breath until I turned blue, and Granny said I was going to hell for being disobedient and Aunt Edna tried to give me mouth-to-mouth, until Mommy stopped her and spared me my first taste of Budweiser.

They sent Uncle Skeeter out to buy another doll, cut off the hair, mark all over the face, run over it a couple of times, and pass it off as my Yucky-Yucky. Please, did they think me an idiot? I may have forgotten the number six every time I counted to ten, but I knew an imposter when I saw one. I let them have a couple moments of peace before launching into another jag of earth-shattering bellows.

It was then that Grunt, Cousin Ned's three-legged, deaf hound dog, caught sight of Yucky-Yucky and went after it—one of those nice unplanned surprises. I cranked it up a notch while they all chased after Grunt to get the doll, knocking over furniture and trashing what was probably already considered trash to begin with. Ned finally pried the plastic doll from Grunt's teeth and threw it to Aunt Vyrnetta, who managed to grab it and fling it up into the air before falling backwards into the fish tank and ripping her new orange Capri pants which, Mommy was correct, made her rear end look like an overgrown pumpkin.

And this is how the counterfeit Yucky-Yucky flew directly into the ceiling fan, which had been operating at full speed ever since Aunt Edna had another one of her hot flashes. And there we all witnessed, with startling clarity, the death of this imposter Yucky-Yucky, who was decapitated in front of our very eyes. Death by ceiling fan.

I stopped crying. The dog stopped barking. Everybody stopped talking and moving at once. Complete silence, except for the sound of the plastic head rolling across the faux hardwood floor where it landed with a thud against a ceramic dolphin wearing sunglasses, the rest of its body still lodged in the fan, whirling round and round like some freaky carnival ride.

They all agreed that letting me stay up as late as I wanted would affect me far less than the scarring that would occur from the gruesome scene which had just played out. And so there I sat, in the middle of it all, for the rest of the night: nestled in my Aunt Edna's bosom that smelled like roses and Marlboros, while Granny prayed over my soul and Uncle Skeet picked a little "I'll Fly Away" on the guitar. Eventually, I fell asleep. Who can blame me? I was exhausted.

And in my dreams I replayed that scene over and over—my first real decapitation. Too cool. How will I ever top that? (End of story)

Some of us have crazy families and crazy people in our lives. And if we're not careful, our time can be spent obsessing about how to deal with people that irritate us. The Bible is right on in that whole "love your neighbor" business, but it is possible to love your neighbors and not let them move in. It is possible to forgive someone and not spend your holidays with them. It is important to set boundaries in life. And sometimes it's important to see life from another perspective.

Tammy worked at the desk behind me at the Fix 'N Stitch Medical Center that summer when I answered phones—that stage of my life where I was trying to find myself, which, by the way, didn't happen until years later, and what I found was less than appealing. Tammy spent all day crunching numbers and the good moods of anybody who crossed her path. She, like the long line of Southern women in her family before her, had made an art out of artificial niceness: the overly exaggerated smile; the pageant wave from across the room; the kisses aimed at the air; the "let's do lunch" that meant anything but.

She was the most dangerous kind of negative person, in that it was hidden underneath layers of sugar-coated compliments and promises. And then when you turned your back—look out. She could ruin reputations in seconds, with nothing more than a simple unspoken implication. She was a master. She had the uncanny ability to suck the positive energy out of everybody in the room without saying a word, all the while claiming to be your best friend. You didn't get the last word—she did. You didn't win—she did. You couldn't reason with her because Tammy did no wrong. Your point had no merit and warranted the same results as reasoning with a drunk. If there was anything blocking our path to creativity and productivity, she was it. Hence the nickname: Toxic Tammy.

We each had our own way of handling Toxic Tammy. May Belle tried to fix her with Jesus. Dustin, who ran errands while he trained to be a motivational speaker, told her stories about lighthouses and starfish and taught her to break a board with her bare hands. Doreen sneezed on her phone and popped some more of mommy's little happy pills that she started taking after her fifth child was born. Barb had a voodoo doll with hair like Tammy's, covered in stick pins, hidden in her bottom drawer. And I had created a space on a social site in her honor, where I had uploaded enlarged photos of her rear end in those checkered Capri pants. It wasn't admirable, but it got us through the day.

So you can imagine our surprise when we found out she was getting married to that bald guy who taught math over at the community college—a man we swore was a good inch taller when they first started dating. And it was an even bigger surprise when we found out we were her bridesmaids. Apparently, we were the only friends she had, with the exception of the two exchange students from Romania. We were Toxic Tammy's bridesmaids—it was hard to fathom—and she didn't take no for an answer. It's hard enough to be in a wedding for someone you like, who has just made you pay $200 for a dress that makes you look like Scarlett O'Hara on crack. But for Tammy? Barb put a wedding gown on her voodoo doll.

For the next six months, Toxic Tammy ordered us around and made sure we never went anywhere without our fifty-page bridesmaid handbook with blank pages in the back for notes. There were four showers, five planning meetings, an engagement cookout, dress fittings, and even a workout regimen to prepare us for our wedding goal weight. Doreen had to renew her prescription three times. Barb had to go buy another voodoo doll after lighting the last one on fire. And May Belle had decided to rethink her views on loving your neighbor.

I won't bore you with all the wedding details and make you have to share the nightmare. But there was one bridal shower that sticks out in my mind even after all these years. It was the one where we met Tammy's mother for the first time. We were intrigued to meet her, much as you would be intrigued to meet the mother of a baby with three heads. For starters, she was breathtakingly beautiful—model beautiful. She was sweet, helpful, and had great taste in clothes. She complimented us and hugged us with a sympathetic smile that said she understood it must be tough working with her daughter. We were wondering how somebody so sweet could have produced somebody so rotten, when we noticed it. Quiet at first—a whispered comment, a turned-up lip, a smile bordering on a snarl. As Tammy's mother grew more comfortable around us, her exterior started to melt.

Tammy opened a casserole dish and her mother snickered. Tammy opened the blanket her cousin stitched, and the mother rolled her eyes. Somebody called her fiancé cute and Tammy's mother smirked. Somebody asked to see the dress and her mother informed us it was a knockoff. Tammy opened up lingerie, and her mother made sure it was an extra large. Right before our eyes, Tammy Toxic shrunk, and we saw her turn into the little girl who knew she'd never be good enough, while her mother turned into the ugliest woman we had ever seen.

The wedding was a nightmare, the dresses even worse, and there were times we could barely hold our tongues. And still, after all we did for her, things stayed the same. Tammy didn't get any nicer after that day. She was just as nasty as before. Nothing had changed. Except us. May Belle stopped working so hard to fix her. Dustin started motivating someone else. Doreen stopped seeking vengeance. I took down the social site. The voodoo doll disappeared. We stopped trying to win. And we learned to let it go. Because somehow, even when it got really bad, we would remember that little girl sitting there cowering under her mother—the little girl who would never be good enough. No, Tammy didn't change. We did. And maybe, just maybe, we were the ones blocking the productivity all along. Because, after all, poison isn't poisonous unless you drink it.

And then there comes a time when we have to cut that friend free—so here are some tips on how to lose a friend in ten days or less. We have enough articles and cute little coffee table books that sing the praises of friendship. But what about that friend we are dying to get rid of? You know the one—don't deny it—the one who at the very mention of her name, your eye starts to twitch. The very sight of her car pulling into your driveway actually has you considering faking your own death. The one who bugs you so bad you can't stand her children just by association. Help is on the way. I have come up with some surefire ways to get rid of unwanted friends.

1. Ask her if she's gained weight. Look closely at her hips and her rear end as if you are trying to solve a mysterious math equation. Tell her it's okay, that we all let ourselves go when we get to that age. And would she consider Botox?

2. Ask her to host a scrapbook party at her house—every time you see her. Then tell her exactly how you want it done and offer to clean her house for her, with a look that says you remember the last time you were there and your kid tripped on one of her dust bunnies. The key here is to look at her like she's a dog with three legs.

3. Call her every day and leave really long messages on her answering machine that always start with, "Oops, the machine just cut me off. Let me finish up. I'll be really quick." Then leave a new phone number at the very end of the message, and say it real fast and mumble it so she can't get it and has to listen to the entire message again.

4. Pop up in her bushes on Thursday morning when she comes out to get the paper. Tell her you were just hanging out.

5. Send her spam emails at least three times a day with videos and pictures attached, with messages telling her to light a candle and pass this on to twenty-five other people in the next twenty-four hours. Accuse her of being the devil's spawn if she doesn't answer. Attaching a virus always helps.

6. Tell her you want to sit down and talk about where she stands spiritually. This one is particularly effective, as it will not only get rid of her—chances are good it will get rid of everyone she knows too.

7. Loan her money or offer to watch her children if she watches yours. Watch her kids and you'll never see her again.

8. Fake your own death. This can be tricky to pull off, but it's a permanent solution.

9. Show her your childbirth video and pause on the placenta while you go answer the phone.

10. And last, but not least, give her a second chance. Take the love-your-neighbor thing seriously. It's easy to love the lovable. But it says even more about your character if you're able to love the unlovable. And, for the record, there's nothing wrong with loving her from far away.

P.S. If you're reading this, you are the good kind of friend: just ignore my picture in the obituary section.

- Set boundaries for the other people in your life
- You don't have to make everyone happy
- Don't feel you have to apologize for the actions of those around you
- Let comments roll off

Discussion Questions:

1. Do you have clear boundaries for friends and extended family? Do they know when it's okay to call and when you need that time for yourself? Don't be afraid to establish some guidelines. Your friends will understand and if they don't, it doesn't matter.

2. It is not your job to make sure everybody in the room is getting along. In meetings, do you find yourself trying to make sure that people don't offend other people?

3. Do you apologize for the actions of those around you? Do you feel like their behavior reflects badly upon you? What

can you do to fix it? Can you really change that person? How can you handle their behavior with love and grace?

4. We can't control other people, but we can control how we react to them. What is the best way to handle a difficult person?

Myth #7   THE BAD GUY ALWAYS DIES

Forgiveness

Don't we love it when the evil villain melts into nothingness, screeching his way to a violent and justified death? Don't we wish real life were that way sometimes? That the bad guy would get it in the end? But you already know that it doesn't work that way. The bad guy often gets away with it and we are never given our moment of justice, our moment of closure. God says He'll take care of it and that we need to turn the other cheek. So how do we forgive those who are so hard to forgive? And why do we forgive those who don't deserve it? Well, we forgive for ourselves, not for them, because carrying the weight of a grudge is unhealthy and stands in the way of our own happiness. Just look what happened in our family one Thanksgiving.

Aunt Edna meant well when she announced—somewhere between *amen* and *please pass the potatoes*—that she was starting a new Thanksgiving tradition, while the rest of us broke out into a unified sweat remembering the last family tradition that had started with a candle and a song, and had ended with a flaming wig, a hairless cat, two empty rolls of duct tape, and a chain of prayer that covered two counties.

Her tradition was beautifully stated—lifted, no doubt, right out of the body of the email chain letter she received that promised everything (short of a monogrammed recliner in heaven) if she followed it and forwarded it to seventy-five friends in twenty-four hours. It went something like this: *In the midst of your Thanksgiving celebrations take the time to leave one symbolic seat open at the table, a seat that each of you will lovingly fill with your most cherished dearly departed relative who has gone on before you and can only attend in spirit. And as you share your thoughts and reflections on the people that each of you have designated for that empty seat, may you find your table filled with memories and blessings and the peace of those who have gone before you.* Yeah, I gagged too the first time I heard it. Had the writer known our family, he would have thought twice about sending that email.

We were asked to bring back lost relatives. Not "lost" as in missing, like Uncle Skeeter, who disappeared after buying lottery tickets and all that remains is his picture on the milk cartons in the Gas 'n Go. Not "lost" as in those of the unsaved nature (note: always whisper the word *unsaved*), who are the primary concern of Aunt Jean's prayer meetings, unless there happens to be something more pressing worth mentioning, like Mildred's husband running off with that overly painted-up hussy with implants who'd come traveling through town with the carnival, bless her heart. But "lost" as in those no longer with us—those who have gone on to claim their winnings in that great lottery in the sky. And so that's how we found ourselves munching on turkey legs and conjuring up dead folks.

Grandpa Jake was brought back, and we remembered riding in the back of his pickup truck. Somebody brought back Old Widow Jenkins and her chocolate chip cookies that could be smelled for weeks. Somebody else brought back Elvis, which sparked a healthy discussion over whether he was really dead or not, and Aunt Bitsy had a moment of silence for whoever invented spandex, taking her from a size eighteen to a size six. Had our family been a little smaller, or less inclined to drink, things would probably have continued to move at a relatively harmonious and harmless pace. But our family is not small, and those who partook in the hooch outnumbered those who didn't, and things started to take an ugly turn.

Gertie brought back her husband Clyde to ask him where the remote control had gone off to, as he was the last person seen with it. Buster brought back an old army buddy and cussed him out for never paying him that fifty dollars he owed him from that poker game, and my cousin Chastity brought back her guidance counselor to let him know she was not in fact destined for a life of hanging on a MOST WANTED poster, but was a respected lounge singer on the Holiday Inn circuit, thank you very much. May Belle's daughter brought back her first-grade teacher to ask her was it true that her oversized bosom hid more than pencils and erasers (an occasional unruly child, as rumor had it), and is that what really happened to her Betsy-Wetsy doll?

Vyrnetta brought back Billie P. Jenkins, who dumped her in the tenth grade in exchange for a freckled redhead from Des Moines who couldn't even twirl a baton, for heaven sakes, and Vyrnetta just wanted to let Billie know that she was so over him. Wynona brought back her dear beloved poodle, Phoebe, who apparently didn't appreciate having been stuffed and placed by the Christmas tree every year, according to Buster, who claimed to have psychic canine powers. Ernestine brought back whoever wrote that song "Feelings," and said they should be shot for that one if they weren't shot already, that it was the worst song she'd ever heard and every time she walked out of an elevator it took her three days to get that blasted tune out of her head and, darn it, now it was back in her head again.

Loretta was muttering to the empty chair about the casserole dish that was never returned, and somebody asked Old Hank why he wasn't bringing back his beloved wife Cheryl, to which he replied that he finally got himself some peace and quiet—why in the world would he want to bring that woman back? Star's boyfriend Hershel said he wanted to bring back Moses, which might have been admirable, but Hershel was about as pious as a sewer rat and was only trying to impress us, which set off Aunt Edna, who claimed that he'd turned our tradition into a blasphemy asking to bring back Moses, and that not a one of us had set aside a seat for Jesus and we were all going to hell.

I'm not sure who threw the first biscuit, or at what point the serving spoon became a weapon to launch Vyrnetta's hash casserole across the room, where it landed with a thud on the oil painting of some distant great aunt, whose scowl grew even larger when she tasted it. Or exactly when Edsel lost his dentures and Bitsy fell rear end into the punch bowl, and Uncle Buford lost his hearing aid in the congealed salad and swore he could hear the fruit cocktail screaming in their gelatin coffins.

At some point, Aunt Edna's well-meaning new tradition had turned into a food fight of divine proportions that ended only when we had run out of food and dead people to bring back. What had started as a simple gesture ended with a whole new set of grudges, a chain of prayer that covered three counties, and an empty seat that sat under a harsh threat of physical violence from Aunt Edna herself should anyone even think about bringing some poor soul back to be around this crazy family, implying that the long-lost relatives were in fact the lucky ones. She's probably right. Maybe next time she'll think twice about sharing those emails.

So when God is talking about forgiving people who annoy you, I can relate. And over the years I've learned to set boundaries and embrace what makes people unique, for people are seldom what they seem. And if you want to get out there and see the people, serve jury duty. (Sorry, this chapter's kind of long, so this might be a good time to take a snack break.)

There are three things I never like to find in my mailbox: an insurance bill, a jury summons, and another invitation to my cousin Fern's Scrapbooking for Jesus party. Last month I received all three. I paid the bill, called Fern and regretfully declined because my neighbor's Jewelry for Jesus party was on the same day, and sat there holding the official red summons with shaking hand, asking, "Why me, Lord? Why me?" And He answered, "Why not you?" And like I had been taught by every motivational speaker since birth, I did an inward attitude reversal and decided to embrace jury duty with the same enthusiasm with which my Aunt Bitsy embraces the all-you-can-eat chicken wing buffet.

Some people don't believe you can prepare for jury duty. I, however, was born for it, having clocked in at six hundred forty-seven episodes of *Law and Order*, *SVU,* and *Criminal Intent*—and four consecutive seasons of *CSI*. Not only have I been educated in all aspects of the law and how to gather evidence wearing high heels and cleavage-inspired T-shirts, but I am also quite confident that I could perform an autopsy upon request—along with a little criminal profiling—all in sixty minutes. The only thing left to do, of course, was to plan my outfit. I went for the animal print clogs with the black slacks that hold in my stomach, and the matching animal print vest which I ditched at the last minute for fear of a stray PETA activist who didn't know her faux. It was undoubtedly the best outfit for serving my civic duty in fashion, and I give full credit to my fashion magazines.

I arrived at the courthouse with a smile (and blisters from running two miles in clogs) and found two lines that ran the length of the building. It was obvious that one line represented those reporting for jury duty, and the other for those in need of a jury. Being that I have a tendency to stereotype, I expected to be able to tell immediately which line was mine. The unfortunate line—those who'd experienced momentary lapses of judgment—would surely be recognized by their pierced and dyed skin, frantic aura of hopelessness, and the blatant fashion "No-Nos" featured every month in fashion magazines, which were the sign (or perhaps the cause) of their life of lawlessness. The other line would consist of Sunday school teachers, well-meaning shop owners, and ordinary people like me.

But I couldn't tell. The suits were in both lines. The wild-eyed fidgeters were on both sides. And I must admit: both sides had good hair. Both lines held people who appeared to have the potential to come unhinged at any moment. I chose the shorter one. Not only was I the only one in line who was smiling, but I had an obvious aura of eagerness about me, much like a puppy waiting for someone to rub his belly. I don't deny it. I was excited, by golly. I was here to serve my country, my eyelashes had no clumps, and this time it wasn't me the cop caught speeding. I was ready to make a difference—as long as it only took one day, because I had a hair appointment the next day. I'm all for serving my duty, but it took me six months to get that appointment and I wouldn't miss it if I had a horrible car accident on the way and they had to use my hairdresser's electrical outlet to charge the paddles to restart my heart. I'm getting my roots done. So I waited patiently in line, hoping my butt didn't look big in those pants since I was on the busiest corner in downtown morning-commute traffic, trying to talk to the tall woman with the unusually large Adam's apple who obviously did not want to be bothered, even if I was going to ask who did her highlights.

Finally we got in and they put us in another room to sit and wait. I headed to the back of the room, like the long line of Baptists before me, and found myself staring at the back of everyone's head, happy to report that the majority of Americans (I can safely say that, since this was a random sample of the population) wash behind their ears. That's when it struck me that I was sitting in a random sample of my community—a statistician's heaven. Here was my opportunity to create my own unending list of stats for my speeches, whereupon (is that still a word?) I could say with confidence, "One out of every ten Americans," with credibility and truth. As irony would have it, I couldn't think of good consumer questions to ask—like buying habits or spending motivations—but whether one out of every ten Americans does in fact prefer Crest over the leading brand.

Have you ever noticed that the clock stops ticking in a jury room? And every minute can feel like ten when you're staring ahead and trying not to make eye contact? The excitement was starting to wear off. We were supposed to start at 8:30. It was 8:55 and we hadn't moved; I had already counted the ceiling tiles twice, dug around my purse for a forgotten piece of chocolate (as if), and planned my escape route should a wayward felon seeking revenge come bursting into our room. Would I drop and play dead, or stand up and profess my faith, willing to take a bullet from the hooded guy who held up a pawn shop? By 9:02 I was wondering if the sales manual would refer to this room full of jurors as a networking opportunity.

Jury duty is a great place to watch people—like the guy whose monogrammed pocket protector spelled HERB, who rapidly scribbled notes on every word the clerk said, and kept asking her to rewind the jury duty video because he didn't catch that last line. Yep, he was shoved in a locker more than once. And the beefy guy beside him who was sound asleep—probably tired from shoving Herb into the locker. There was the impatient woman who sighed every three minutes as if to remind us all that there were seventy-five other places she needed to be, each of which was infinitely more important than ours. And the sweet little old lady who had nowhere else to go and would we like some of her homemade fudge she got up an extra hour early to make?

There was the pasty bald guy with the twitch who looked like he was going to pass out at any moment, and the young bling-covered kid wearing headphones and bobbing his head, either to Mendelssohn's *Concerto in G* or "Pimp Your Mamma," the instrumental version. The guy who glared as if daring anybody to talk to him, and the one who whipped out his Bible; resulting in an immediate ten-foot clearance as people fled from him like he had typhoid fever and had just coughed without covering his mouth. And not to forget the sweet little man who parked in the spot marked RESERVED because he thought it was reserved for him—bless his heart—and the one who sat there for five hours before he realized he was there on the wrong day. And the one who kept trying to prove to the clerk that he had a mental disability and should be excused, when it was quite obvious the lady beside me, who was talking to her purse, had the true disability. It seemed that I was the only normal person there, which explains why nobody commented on my cute clogs, except for the lady talking to her purse, who tried to pet them. If that was a jury of my peers, then I need to move. And please explain to me the logic behind the clerk's announcement: "Anyone who does not speak English may now be excused." The same logic, obviously, that is behind the sign that says: NO SEEING EYE DOGS.

There was the whole having-to-pee incident that happened at 9:13. Not the most life-threatening dilemma, but a typical example of how I can take the mundane and beat it to death. I had already planned my morning accordingly, to allow for several stops before getting to the courthouse. I didn't drink anything after 7:00 A.M., just to be sure. But now it's 9:13 and I'm wondering if I should go, despite the fact that I don't have to. But what if I go now and they call my number? What if I can't hear them over the flush and everybody is in the jury room wondering what happened to number 342, and they have to page me and call in the dogs who follow the scent of Suave and lead everyone to stall number one—which, for the record, is supposed to be the cleanest one, because people always avoid the first one thinking it will be the most used, so it turns out to be the least used, until we start spreading the word at which point the theory dies, and maybe that's happened already because I've told a LOT of people. No, I shouldn't go now. I should wait. But what if I sit here only to find they aren't going to call my number for another hour and then I really have to go, but then I can't go because surely they will be close to calling my number then? What if I don't go at all and I'm sitting in the jury box missing everything they're saying because my bladder has ruptured and I'm too scared to interrupt, and I vote for convicting the guy because it will be faster? I decided to go and felt that my decision was the right one. I returned in three minutes and found that nothing had occurred in my absence.

So I just sat there and experienced that rare feeling of having absolutely nothing to do but sit and be. It occurred to me that I couldn't remember the last time I sat like this and really felt my own existence. No emails to answer, no laundry, no fishing a toy out of a toilet. Nothing to do but sit, relax, breathe, and get in touch with my inner core. Turns out there's not much to my inner core, and by 9:30 I had determined that sitting is overrated.

And then it happened. Just kidding. Nothing happened. For two hours. Not a bleep. For three hours, for four hours. Nothing but a couple of breaks and then more waiting. In our fast-paced world of technology and craziness, we were all forced to go into an adult time-out: to sit in a quiet room, stare at a stone wall as we acted out our civic duty, and then go home. And even though the whole day passed with no shouts for justice or reenacted scenes from *Twelve Angry Men*—even though I did not get to carve a cadaver or hold up a spec of dust under a light bulb—I still came away from that experience a little different than when I went in.

Being in that room reminded me that sometimes people aren't what they seem—turns out Mr. Bling with the headphones was listening to motivational tapes, and the little old fudge lady was once an erotic dancer in Des Moines. I was reminded that we live in a place where people come together in the face of crisis—no matter what we look like or our views on capital punishment. Someone slips in the hallway and we all run to help. And I was reminded that even in something as dreary as jury duty, there's always a funny side. You just have to know where to look.

- Thicken up your skin. There are always going to be people who will have a problem with what you say or do, or the way you look. Forget about it. You have a choice in how you react. Exercise this choice early in the confrontation. Don't take their words, opinions, or facial gestures personally. Let it stay their problem, not yours. Let them keep the unhealthy stress. Why should you risk having a heart attack while they walk off whistling and stress free?

- Let it go. So what if she said your rear end looks like two pigs fighting under a blanket? Let it go—without running to tell twenty other people.

- Embrace what makes other people unique. So what if she interrupts everybody? So what if he starts every story with what he had for breakfast? So what if she whistles through her nose or if he always has to have the last word? Let him have it.

- Some of the most annoying people can turn out to be your greatest treasures. Give people a chance. Then give them a second one.

- Forgive. Release your anger because holding on to it will only hurt you, not them. You don't have to seek them out, embrace them, or even release them of their obligations. Just forgive them. And you don't have to go tell them you forgive them. That's just your sneaky way of getting the last word.

Discussion Questions:

Difficult people are one of the biggest challenges we face—especially the people that you are forced to be around every day. Is there someone giving you grief? Have you talked about this with her in a civilized way? Have you set boundaries? Have you tried to fix the situation or are you just talking about it? Is it time to just let it go—even when you have to face them again?

Myth #8   THE WIZARD WAS A FAKE

Where do you find your truth?

What a bummer to go all that way down the yellow brick road wearing tight red shoes that don't match your outfit, only to find out this wonderful wizard you've been hearing about is a fraud. Now *that's* realistic. We are all in search of something that helps life make sense. A truth we can hold on to. That set of core beliefs to which we hold ourselves accountable. We don't agree on the details, but we all agree that there is more to life than the view from where we sit. You have to acknowledge that there is a higher power that has more control than you do. Spend some time thinking about the big picture. Find that one thing you have to hang on to that is bigger than your stuff; bigger than your circumstances; bigger than your friends and their opinions. Truth is not relative. Which, of course, reminds me of a story.

Yes, it happened again, this time to my Cousin Nester, who called us all up this morning to say that Jesus had appeared on the side of his garage—not in the flesh, or even in the vapor, but in a distorted image on wood apparently made from rust, sap, and an unidentifiable white substance most likely blamed on birds and the adjacent cherry tree. Nester didn't believe in Jesus, but was willing to bet his lottery ticket that this was in fact the HOLY OF HOLIES who had taken residence above his trash cans, staring down with a look of disdain at the collection of assorted hubcaps and the discarded recliner bearing the imprint of Nester's butt.

Nester took this sighting to mean two things: the recliner should stay, and here was the new business opportunity he'd been waiting for. And with more ambition than he had shown in his combined forty-five years, he notified the press, alerted the neighbors, slapped up a sign that said $10 TO SEE JESUS, set up an eBay account, and put his son Dudley to work scraping pieces of wood off the side of the garage to sell to the highest bidders.

So if you walked past Nester's house this morning, that's why you saw all the cameras and the large gathering of curious faces cocked to the side in rapt attention, intent on getting their full ten dollars' worth. It was the first time Jesus had been sighted in their town (outside the stained-glass and shrink-wrapped variety, and the time Granny Jean mixed up her medications) so it was not something to be taken lightly. People gave it the piety deserving of a savior, no matter where they fell on the scale of belief, for even the most critical unbeliever figured it prudent to be respectful, just in case. They were all eager to speak about the miracle to the TV cameras shoved in their faces, happy to be asked about something other than a tornado or beauty pageant queen gone bad.

It was Vyrnetta who first brought into question the authenticity of this spiritual sighting, pointing out that she saw in a magazine that he was just spotted yesterday in a grilled cheese sandwich in Idaho, and this magazine should know, being as they were the first to show pictures of J-Lo's babies. And Booker Diggs made a very good argument that while the image could be perceived as Jesus, it bore a more striking resemblance to Sonny Bono. And how come whenever images appeared like this, people immediately assumed it was Jesus? And if Jesus was coming back, why would he pick the side of the garage? Why would he pick that town, for that matter? Good grief, they didn't even have a McDonald's. To which Mildred Jenkins pointed out that the first time he came it was as a carpenter born in a stable, and nobody argued with Mildred, who'd been teaching Sunday school since she was five.

Pastor Fern came over and dramatically announced that it couldn't be the real thing, because sightings of this nature only appeared to those who attended church, Sunday school, and served on at least two committees. He was followed by Father Jim, the priest, who wasn't really a priest, but had started out to be one before he got a calling to go into country music, and he said that it couldn't be considered real until somebody sprinkled some holy water on it. Bitsy offered up some of the special tonic she carried in her purse that, despite her protests, smelled an awful lot like moonshine. She said it was to help calm her nerves and that should count as holy, because nothing could work a miracle like that stuff. Ernestine claimed that was downright blasphemy and didn't it just figure, coming from a Presbyterian. This resulted in a verbal assault on the Baptists, which resulted in a hit on two Methodists, four Mormons, and one suspected heathen, which opened the door for the other denominations present until no one was left unscathed.

Bucky said this was a sure sign that they were all going to hell, and he started confessing a list of sins that, while entertaining, were probably better left private. The Tucker twins were singing and throwing their hands up in the air, hoping to signal up a revival, when things turned from the verbal to the physical as Buster punched Nester and both of them fell back against the garage. And in one fell swoop the Jesus image was gone—smeared like a child's finger painting, which now looked more like Courtney Love. They all froze, pondering the ramifications of having erased Jesus. This couldn't be good. If his appearance was a sign, imagine what erasing him could mean. And they found themselves standing in a moment equivalent to that of a frat party when the keg's run dry. And so they went their separate ways, some giving this Jesus thing a little more thought, and others quickly distracted by the yard sale two doors down. It was Mildred Jenkins who stood there a little longer than everyone else, staring at the side of the garage and shaking her head at the mystery—not the mystery of a face made out of rust, but the mystery that so many would go to such great lengths to find him when he's been right here all along.

- Find something bigger to hang on—bigger than your stuff, bigger than your circumstances, bigger than your relationships, and bigger than other people's opinions. You spend a lot of time protecting your belongings and your computer files. Why not spend a little time on this?

Discussion Question:

What do you have to hang on to that you can never lose?

Myth #9 IT'S ALL ABOUT THE PRINCE

No, he doesn't complete you

Why is it that in fairy tales the answer is always found in a kiss from a charming prince? Now I've got nothing against kisses, but good grief, we're putting a lot of pressure on Prince Charming, aren't we? I have a hard time imagining a ten-car pileup on the highway, with mass hysteria, traffic backed up for miles with no hope in sight until, wait—what is that?—is that a white horse? I do believe it is. A white horse charging through the traffic. And, could it be? Yes! I do believe it is a charming prince brandishing his sword. And could his lips be puckered? Why, yes, they are. Praise be! He's here. He's here.

It's no wonder that so many women grow up thinking that they're not normal unless they have a charming prince; that their life doesn't start until he comes along; that he will fill all their empty places and make them whole. I got news. Your significant other's job is not to complete you. It is not his sole purpose to make you happy and content. That's your job. You need to be complete before that man gets here. And you need to stop trying to turn your relationship into a fairy tale. It's real life. And one day that prince has to come down off of that horse and pop open a coke in front of the football game. Just look what happened to Nadine and Buster.

Nadine and Buster met at a tractor pull twenty years ago. I remember when Nadine was having a time getting Buster to take out the trash. She tried everything. Asked him nicely and he'd say, "Yes, dear," and then he'd forget. She'd leave him little notes and he wouldn't see them. She'd put the trash by the front door and he'd go out the back. Finally she let the trash pile so high you had to lean *up* to throw anything away, and he'd spend twenty minutes trying to work that last piece in.

Until, like happens to us all, something little turned into something bigger, and Nadine began to wonder what it would be like to have a man who took out the trash. And maybe one who actually cooked on occasion. And while she was at it, one who brought her flowers and didn't spend all his time out in that shed out back.

And eventually, over time the dream got bigger and the reality got smaller, until that one Saturday morning when the trash had piled up again, and Nadine decided she'd had enough. It was time. She had read all the books, talked to all her divorced friends, and watched a couple of episodes of *Oprah* to get her courage up. And she marched out back to the shed to tell Buster it was over, muttering to herself, sidestepping old tires, rusty car parts, and the three lawn mowers he had promised to fix five years ago—all proof of a life she no longer wanted.

She threw open the door to the shed and tried to adjust her eyes to the dim light coming from the one bulb hanging by a chain in the middle of the dark shed. Buster was caught off guard. She'd never been in his shed before. And just as her mouth was forming the words *Buster, it's over,* she froze as the object behind Buster came into focus. It was, of all things, a china cabinet, half finished. It was perfect: handmade, sanded and stained, flowers etched into each of the drawers. Adjustable shelves. For the first time in Nadine's life, she was speechless, tears streaming down her face.

Well, said Buster, *you said you always missed that china cabinet of your great grandmother's that got ruined in the flood. I took all the old pictures and had 'em blown up so's I could see how it was. It was supposed to be ready last Christmas. You don't have to use it if it's not nice enough.*

But Nadine wasn't listening. She couldn't hear over the sound of her heart healing. And in that moment, Nadine's dream faded into her reality as she stared at the man she then quietly vowed to love until death. In that moment Nadine learned that marriage, just like life, doesn't always promise happily-ever-afters. Or maybe it does; she just needed to know where to look.

- Release unrealistic expectations of what your relationship should be—of what your spouse should be
- It is not your significant other's role to complete you—you need to do that on your own first

Discussion Questions:

- Do you feel like your fairy tale has turned into some low-budget clearance-table DVD?

- What do you think a marriage should be like? Is this realistic?

- Do you find yourself thinking that you'd be happy if he/she would just...?

- For those of you who aren't married: Do you feel like you're just hanging in limbo? That you missed out on the good ride?

- What is it that you think stands in the way of your peace? And do you think someone else is responsible for putting it there?

- People show love and affection in many ways. We're so busy looking for the type of love we expect to receive that we often miss the love others give. That's what happened with Nadine and Buster. Discuss.

Myth #10   YOU'VE ALWAYS GOT A FAN CLUB

Create a strong support group

Oh, were it that easy—just wake up in a problem and within minutes you have a lion, a tin man, and a scarecrow ready to drop everything and travel down that yellow brick road with you. The fairy-tale prince and princess always have an endless supply of furry little creatures that have nothing else to do but help them accomplish their dreams. I once stared at my hamster every night for three weeks, waiting for it to turn into a carriage. And we won't even talk about the whole frog-in-biology incident that did not result in a charming prince, but did make my lips taste like formaldehyde for weeks. In our crazy world of technology and busyness (if it's not a word, it should be) and the eternal quest to do more, friends come and go through our lives like movie rentals, and we can get so wrapped up in our own chaos that when we really need them, our friends are gone. And we find ourselves wanting to call up Sue for dinner and a movie and find that Sue can't come because she has three kids now and an acting career. And we find that while we have five hundred online friends, we're lonely. And it's our own fault.

Finding friends and keeping them is hard work, and while we may not have as much time as we did before real life set in, we still have to put work into our friendships if we want to depend on them when it matters. You are only as lonely as you want to be. There is nothing to get you through the tough times like a group of friends who know the real you and like you anyway. Just be careful not to set unrealistic expectations on your friends. There is nothing more dangerous than two friends who have different definitions of friendship. Find friends whose schedules are similar to yours. Find friends with common shared experiences. Find friends who like to do what you like to do. But most of all, find friends that you can go to the restroom with. If you are a man, have you ever wondered why women go to the bathroom in pairs? Well, I'm going to tell you. But then I'll have to kill you. We go the bathroom in pairs because:

You need someone to talk to in line about how you can't believe she wore that dreadful thing out of the house; that he had the nerve to tell that joke; how shocked you are that she has put on all that weight since you saw her last; can you believe the price of red bell pepper; and that this morning you found a lump. And even though you just met her, she will understand.

You need her to affirm that the waiter did in fact wink at you at the salad bar, and that you didn't have that much bread (those were little pieces after all), and that it would be better to start the diet tomorrow, and that it was only a small glass of wine—everybody slurs on occasion. And she'll tell you the lump is probably nothing.

You need someone to stand beside you when you look in the mirror and chastise yourself at how fat you've gotten, so she can adamantly protest and tell you it's only the lighting and wherever did you get that precious vest, whereupon in three seconds you give her a rundown of the store, the exact moment you purchased it, the feeling you got when you saw it, and what it cost down to the penny.

You need somebody to help look under the doors for feet, to stand in front of the inevitable door that never fully closes, and someone to hold your purse, coat, cell phone, umbrella, half-eaten popcorn, and Diet Coke.

There won't be any toilet paper, so you need someone to hand you some from underneath and comment on how disgraceful that a restroom would not have any toilet paper, and those shoes are just precious, did you find them the same day you found the vest?

You need someone to show you how to use the automatic sink, hand you a paper towel, roll eyes with at the lady who didn't wash her hands, and tell you that the back of your hair has a flat spot in it.

You need someone with you when you run into your ex-boyfriend's wife, so you can hear that you are definitely prettier.

You need someone to make sure you don't have lipstick on your teeth, toilet paper on your shoe, or any sort of wardrobe malfunction that wasn't planned. And before you walk out, you need her to look you in the eyes and tell you that everything is going to be okay.

And, finally, you need someone to smile smugly at over dinner because now you've shared one of the rituals that makes us women and turns strangers into friends. And that's why we go to the restroom in pairs. I think the real question we should ask is, why do men go alone?

- You are only as lonely as you want to be
- Cultivate a strong network of friends you can count on
- Find friends with common interests and circumstances
- Establish boundaries

Discussion Questions:

1. Do you have some good friends that you can count on when the going gets tough?

2. Are you there for your friends?

3. Do you cultivate those relationships and work them into your priorities?

4. What are some simple ways that you can be a better friend?

5. If you don't have friends, make a list of places where people like you hang out. Make a concerted effort to put yourself in situations where you can make friends. Do you try to make friends or do you wait for them to come to you?

Myth #11 YOU CAN BE ANYTHING

Sorry, but no you can't

No matter how many verses of "It's a small world" and "When you wish upon a star" you throw at me, no matter how many times you wave that magic wand, no matter how many times I click my heels, I will never be *anything* I want to be. If I could be anything I wanted to be, I would be riding elephants in the circus and married to Slash, a sixth grader who wore parachute pants with zippers on the side, smelled like wet cigarettes, and could burp the alphabet. If I could be anything, I would be a size zero, with abs of steel and no hair on my chin, eating chocolate that never made me gain weight. I'm pretty sure I've reached my full potential. But that sure hasn't stopped me from trying to be something I'm not. Like when I bought those stilettos. You have just got to hear this. Run to the restroom first because this one's funny.

I ordered these new stilettos in the mail because the model looked great wearing them and I was convinced they were the very thing I needed to complete me. Well, that and the sheer shawl with the beaded butterflies. The stilettos, just like the model, were everything I wasn't. They even sounded cool: *stilettos.* I wasn't sure what that meant, but I figured with a name like that they must come with a dark exotic man holding a platter of margaritas.

I should probably tell you that I am not a delicate woman. I bought a bikini this summer and never could get my entire stomach tucked into it—kept popping out on all sides like canned biscuits. Looked like I was wearing an inner tube, and the bottom half of the bikini disappeared from view completely. Now that I think about it, putting stilettos on me made as much sense as putting an alarm system in a Dodge Dart. Yeah, now that I think about it, they weren't me. But that had never stopped me before and it didn't stop me now. Plus, they were only $25.99. And it is a rare day that I can turn down something that's only $25.99, whether I need it or not.

When they arrived, they turned out to be slightly higher than I had pictured—kind of like Great Aunt Ethel gets slightly off balance when she's had seven gin and tonics in the course of an hour. Four inches high. So high, that when I wore them they pitched me forward with every step, and I could actually feel the formation of hairline fractures (not sure that's what they're called, but it sounded good when House said it) along with the whispered cries of my ankles begging for mercy.

Oh, but my calves looked good. And I pictured that model in the catalog and remembered that dream where I saw myself sitting in my future, wearing cardigans and orthopedic tennis shoes and yelling at my afternoon soaps. And I entered into another one of those moments where I break from reality (like when I lost three pounds and thought I could pull off that tube top), and said what I often say when my purchases don't make sense: *I can make these work.*

So every morning I practiced walking in them. And being the practical stay-at-home working mom that I am, I made smart use of my time by breaking in my new shoes while I answered my emails (ah, the joys of working from home) and allowed for my spray self-tanner to set in. This was in the midst of another lapse from reality where I was convinced I wasn't really bright orange, but rather one application away from looking like the model on the bottle. And everybody knows you have to let the stuff dry before you get dressed, so I had on this really little skimpy nightie that was so ugly that my husband referred to it as my "rape prevention outfit"—light blue and covered with tacky orange sunflowers that had been a gift from my great granny, who had one just like it. And come to think of it, she'd never been attacked either. My two-year-old was napping.

Blame it on the delivery guy, but that's how it started when he rang the bell to deliver my new CD box set, *Six Steps to Uncover the New You,* which he apparently thought was a good purchase after taking in my nightie, orange skin, stilettos, and head full of pink sponge rollers. In fact, I think he was a little afraid because he sort of threw the package on the steps and left without even asking for a signature, making me have to walk outside to get it, pitching forward in my new stilettos with every step, like a chicken, while he gunned the engine and peeled off down the street.

That's how I got locked out of the house and found myself standing on the front porch, in that one moment of slow-motion sanity, thinking to myself *this can't be good* before I hit full-fledged panic. The kind of panic that comes with knowing you've just locked yourself outside while your kid is napping inside, intensified by the knowledge that you are standing in front of God and all your neighbors wearing stilettos and a nightie that barely covers the crucial parts and leaves the rest open to the elements, especially the neighbor's dog, who was already drooling at the sight of my plump thigh. Apparently, he didn't care how orange it was.

I ran like a deranged colt to the neighbor's house. No answer. To the other neighbor's house. No answer. Until I had tried almost every house on the street except for the lady who borrowed my heating pad and never returned it. That wound still had not healed. My only recourse was the gas station on the corner. And so there I was, clucking my way down Sherwood Street, looking like a defective dollar-store mannequin in the middle of morning commute traffic, getting a lot of stares, one open-mouthed gape from a freckled kid on a bike, and an occasional honk from a well-meaning trucker taking pity on me, all the while trying my best to look normal.

I pretended like it was nothing out of the ordinary when I half-ran, half-limped past Little Mouse Daycare and waved to the forty-seven faces plastered to the chain link fence with expressions that said this was way better than when Jimmy threw up in the fish tank. I shuffled past Diamond City, where the line of Vietnamese nail technicians waved cheerily and asked, did I need my eyebrows waxed? At least that's what I think they were asking—that or it was some ritual chant to ward off evil, orange, spray-tanned spirits with stilettos. I passed the little Baptist Church on the corner where a group of ladies chatting outside huddled up and started praying for me right there on the spot.

I passed all these places, never once considering that one of them might have a phone I could use—including the corner bakery, where I smiled and, for the first time in my life, kept on going. Okay, okay. So I stopped and got two bear claws and a crème puff. Sue me! I was stressed and I needed the extra energy for the last fifteen feet to the gas station. Only I never made it to the gas station, thanks to the Barney Fife wannabe who pulled me over on the side of Sherwood, just an arm's length away from the pay phone.

Long story short, I was picked up for something that had to do with indecent exposure. They wanted to get me for prostitution but decided that even streetwalkers know better than to put those colors together. And they are trying to get me in the police car and I'm hysterically screaming, "My baby! My baby!" and they think I'm talking in code, perhaps signaling my more dangerous street boss—an obvious conclusion for two hometown cops who'd seen one episode of *Law and Order* too many, and they reach for their tasers, or maybe it was just a breath mint, but I tend to get worked up over things. And just as I'm screaming, *Don't tase me bro', don't tase me,* I see my husband driving up the street.

I swear I saw him hesitate before stopping. He denies it, but I saw the look—the look that said he was trying to decide which was worse: my wrath, or admitting to the cops that we were bound together in matrimony. And like the good man that he is, he talked Officer Fife out of giving me a ticket and threw me in the front seat of his car with a look that dared me to say one word. He didn't want my side of the story. Never did let me tell it.

Now I use the stilettos to hammer stuff, which irritates my husband, who says it's an awfully expensive hammer, and one that brings back stinging memories whenever I pull it out. Apparently, a couple of his golfing buddies happened to see the picture on the front page of the paper with the headline that said: LOCAL WOMAN GIVES STREETWALKERS A BAD NAME.

But I'm all about finding the good in things. And I think there's something to be found in that story. A message. Because don't we all find ourselves at some time in our lives trying to shove our foot into a shoe that doesn't fit? Trying to be something we're not? So learn from me when I say that life was meant to be lived just the way we are. Embrace what makes you unique. Or you might find yourself clucking down the street like a chicken.

- You can't be anything you want to be
- Accept who you are and embrace it

Discussion Questions:

1. Are you still trying to be something you're not? Do you feel at times like this isn't the real you? Who is the real you?

2. Make a list of the things that you will never be. Then let it go.

3. Make a list of the things that you are. Embrace it. These are your gifts and they have value in the great patchwork quilt of life.

Myth #12 SUFFERING IS BAD

Oh, but how would we ever grow?

Sometimes we think the only point to suffering is to get through it, but I think that sometimes it is the very vehicle used to grow us. While we may not like it, suffering is a necessary part of life. I will not try to explain why it is there, only that we can somehow learn to find value in it.

I recently said good-bye to an old friend—my car. A car that I purchased brand new and literally drove to the end of its life. I will not tell you what kind of car, because I am well aware that to some out there it may be funny and shameful, but to others, it would be a step up. It had reached the point where the odometer had started over, and the accessories were worth more than the car itself. The windows could go down, but they couldn't go back up again, which explains why I went with the windblown look back in 2000. The radio cut off and on intermittently. It took me a year to realize that Tim McGraw doesn't have a speech impediment. My car was not a status symbol when new; at the end of its life, it was much like a hunched old man whose only claim to fame was the one time he almost met Elvis's cousin at a truck stop. I will miss that car, and I'll tell you why.

The CHECK ENGINE light had been on for two years and taught me to live life to the fullest, because I was never sure when it might blow up. May I always remember that life is short and to live as if my check engine light is on.

I tried plugging in a GPS, which made as much sense as putting an alarm system on a Dodge Dart. When I plugged the GPS in, it said in a sarcastic tone, "Please. Why even bother? Surely you're not going to take this thing out in public." May I always remember to be proud of the car I drive and the house I live in: Life is too short to be spent comparing ourselves to others.

By the time I paid somebody to take that car, it was lined in petrified French fries, faded M&M's, and possibly a dead body underneath the seat in that place where I could never reach. May I always remember that when all is said and done, clean carpets and windows with no smudges are boring.

That car carried me from single to married, from unemployed to employed to self-employed, from the party life to the responsible life, from floundering to faith. May I always treasure the past as part of who I am and what brought me here, but be courageous enough to let it go.

Nobody ever tried to steal my car (even the time I put a note on it begging for someone to take it) or even looked inside to see if there was something worth stealing. In fact, thieves would often pass my car and leave *me* change. May I always remember that my possessions are just that—possessions. And when all is said and done, they don't matter.

I never had to spend a lot on gas when I went out with my friends, because nobody ever wanted me to drive. And when I took trips, it was a real gas saver because whenever I drove it somewhere, chances were good it would break down and I wouldn't have to drive it back. I was so close with the tow truck company that the driver had me in his wedding at the water park. And the car had been paid off for five years, which was great considering the repairs cost more than the monthly payment. And it doesn't matter if your car gets keyed—who would notice? And what's the point in washing it? Isn't that like buying the bearded lady a new dress? May I remember that nobody has a life without troubles, and sometimes we can find adventures in places we least expect.

Now I have a new car. A sports car? No. A luxury sedan? No. Anything that would boost my credibility? No. It's safe, it's new, it's clean, and it gets me from A to B. And I love it. And I still park at the back of the parking lot and take up two spaces, because this car has to last me until I die.

But I haven't forgotten my old car and the rite of passage attached to it. That car taught me to appreciate the journey, not the destination. Good-bye old car: Rest in peace.

I also think it's important to be careful what you wish for, because one day you may look back and wish desperately for what you had. I am in that stage of parenting that they never warned me about. Okay, so maybe they did warn me. I just didn't listen. That stage they so laughingly refer to as "The Terrible Twos," only my child is four and not so terrible. But still. It's that stage where you engage in countless conversations from the second you wake up until the second you close your eyes at night, and if you want to be truthful, even in your sleep. "What kind of conversations?" you of the childless persuasion ask. Every kind of conversation, from *do you want apple juice or grape juice? the pink cup or the orange cup? the plate with the bear or the plate with the train? be still so I can zip your pants; don't whine; don't you dare hit mommy! that sign says* STOP; *Mommy is a girl and Daddy is a boy; Nana can't come pick you up today; no, tomorrow we go to the zoo;* to *I've told you that we don't pick our nose in public.* When you're a parent nothing is off limits, and it's guaranteed that your child will outlast you every time—unless you sedate him, and even then there's no guarantee.

I remember when our house was a place of solace, with lit candles and Enya crooning softly from a radio not covered with Sponge Bob stickers. Not anymore. Now the house actually shakes with his endless marching in his favorite cowboy boots. He's jumping on beds and throwing things into the sink while he "helps" me clean the kitchen. He shrieks with joy every time Daddy or the UPS man comes (we won't reveal who gets the louder shrieks). He's singing "Jesus Loves Me" in the bathtub and the cartoons are blaring as we bribe him to get dressed. Our house is never quiet, even when my child is not in it, for he undoubtedly leaves random toys behind that he has instructed to go off at a moment's notice from behind a couch or a chair when I'm alone in the shower. The noise of my child carries into the car, the grocery store, the auto shop, the doctor's office. I can't remember the last time I experienced complete and total silence. Until today.

Today while my child was at preschool, I decided not to run errands. I decided not to have my hair cut or my nails done. Instead I went to my mother's house—the closest place I could find to the school—to avoid wasting one second of beloved "me time" driving. I chose to go to my mother's empty house and write. Or at least that's what I told people. I was really going just to sit and be. To drink in the delicious taste of silence. And that's what I did. At first it was nice. Really nice. And I drank enough of it to last me at least until he's four. It was quiet. Really quiet. I tried to hear something and couldn't. No whir of a distant lawn mower. No air conditioner sputtering. No ice dropping in the freezer. Just a faint ticking clock, which I say doesn't count, and was probably just something loose rattling inside my head.

After a while though, it became too quiet. After a while, I really started to feel what a house sounds like when the children are gone and the toys are shipped off. When the fingerprints are no longer on the door handle and the nose prints have been wiped off the glass. No tiny shoes and socks strewn in the hall. No mysterious items found in toilets and drains. Everything in its place. No more conversations. No sign that children were ever here. And you know what? It made me sad. Because it gave me a taste of what life will be like one day when my son has moved away. It reminded me that every day with my shrieking four-year-old is a blessing, and that one day I will look up and have my quiet house, and will probably give anything for one of these days back again.

- Find the value in every situation
- You might look back on this and realize *this* was when you had it good
- Appreciate what you have in the middle of your suffering

Discussion Questions:

1. Is there something about your life that makes you embarrassed? Some area where you feel inferior to your friends?

2. Think about your friends. Do you like them because of where they live or what they have? Do you care where they work?

3. What is the beauty to be found in times of scarcity?

Myth #13   SO YOU THINK YOU'RE A PRINCESS?

Be careful, you might actually be the wicked witch

Isn't it funny how we watch fairy tales and associate with the main character? Of course I'm Cinderella. I'm the pretty sweet one who got the raw deal. We all think we are the princess or the superhero, when there's a chance we might actually be the wicked witch. It's important that we constantly look in the mirror and be honest about who is looking back.

As I wrote this chapter I tried to think of an example where I thought I was the princess, but, as it turned out, I was the witch. And I thought, and I thought. And for the life of me, I couldn't find an example of myself as the witch. Plain and simple, I've always been the sweet one that everybody loves. Surely I'm not a good example of the wicked witch, but I can easily think of plenty of others who are. Like every roommate I've ever had.

I have had twenty-seven roommates in the course of my life, and it's the strangest phenomenon, but every roommate I have ever had has been incredibly annoying. There was the girl I roomed with at piano camp who slept with thirty-seven stuffed animals and sang Barry Manilow songs in her sleep. There was the violin player freshman year of college who liked to light things on fire, and the girl who played hockey and covered her side of the room with yellow sticky notes covered in motivational words of encouragement. There was the one you could hear chewing all the way down the hall and the neat freak who ate soap.

There was the girl who smoked clove cigarettes and wrote poems about a boyfriend she didn't have, and the one who cried on the front porch in the middle of the night while she strummed her guitar. There was the loud talker, the heavy breather, the slob, nail biter, the girl who swore that in her past life she operated the Ferris wheel at the fair, and the one who saw dead people who all looked like Dustin Hoffman. It seems hard to believe that anybody would have such a run of bad luck, like I've had with roommates. And then it hit me. The one thing that all of these roommates had in common— the one person who was at the scene of the crime every time—was me. They weren't the problem; I was. Shocking, I know. I was the wicked witch who had set an expectation so high that nobody could possibly meet it. And somewhere out there are twenty-seven girls who still remember that one roommate they had that was so unbearably hard to live with.

- You may think you're the princess, but sometimes you're actually the witch
- Be willing to look in the mirror and face who is looking back

Discussion Questions:

What about you? Are there ever times when you are the witch? Have you ever thought that maybe they aren't the problem—you are?

Myth #14 JUST WISH UPON A STAR

And then get to work 'cause it ain't that easy

In so many fairy tales all you have to do is link arms and break into song and fears are conquered and obstacles are climbed. Just follow the trail of bread crumbs and you've found your way home. We live in a world where too many people are expecting the easy way out—where we want the payoff but we don't want to work to get it. We want fast answers to our problems. Take diets for instance. We all know what to do to lose weight—eat less and work out more—and any one of us could come up with a diet that would ensure weight loss. But that's not what we want. We want the fast fix without having to put in the time and the effort. Quit expecting your problems to be solved in a day. It doesn't work that way. Some problems took years to develop—so don't think they can be fixed by lunch. Relationships take work. Careers take work. Life takes work. Being a mom takes work. Even talking about it takes work. I'm out of breath.

Today I decided to have a moment of spontaneity with my toddler, which is unusual for me—to engage in things I can't spell. Usually I like my spontaneous moments to occur on weekends, not during those precious work hours when I could be sitting by the phone waiting for it to ring. But when Junior asked me for the hundred and forty-seventh time if he could "do bubbles," I stopped typing, looked up, and much to his surprise and mine, said yes, and we ran outside before I could change my mind.

No coats. No shoes. No sunscreen. We just ran out into the glorious sunshine and, despite that moment where I tripped down the stairs, it was like a scene right out of a movie. Until we started arguing over the bubbles: Who was going to hold the jar? Who was going to blow? Who would get to eat the half-eaten candy bar we found on the ground? And what started as a sweet mommy-and-me project of love and togetherness that belonged on the cover of *Good Mommy* Magazine, quickly spiraled into a DEVIL-MOMMY SPANKS KID IN FRONT YARD moment that belonged on the cover of *Moms Who Shouldn't Be* Magazine. So much for my sweet-lady-next-door image which, according to my husband, disappeared a long time ago—somewhere between the time I threw a pot roast at him as he ran to his car and the time I accidentally posted my labor pictures on MySpace.

And so our bubble-blowing fiasco ended as quickly as it had begun when Junior spilled the entire bottle of bubble liquid on the ground, which left us with nothing to do but just sit. At least that was my plan: to lounge under the oak tree, his head resting on my lap, as I read him excerpts from articles I had written. His plan was to sprint down the driveway and, in rapid succession, collide into the car (yeah, I'm thinking trade school); see which bricks on the side of the house were loose; dig for worms; and lick bark, all of which he found great delight in while my rear end lost feeling on the cold cement porch; my eyes itched; the wind kept blowing my hair into my lip gloss; I got a bug in my teeth; I was reminded of everything in the yard that needs to be done; and I swear I could hear the whisper of missed opportunities on the breeze. Then the rabid squirrel jumped out of a bush and sent both of us running into the house in a fit of hysterics. I probably shouldn't have pushed Junior down on my way to the front porch.

We were both sticky with bubble juice and had to break routine and take a bath in the afternoon (no, not together, they won't let me do that anymore), and I was so worn out that I crawled into bed with him at naptime—the rest of my work day ruined. No emails answered, no phone calls returned. And he curled up against me, his hair still wet from his bath, his arm thrown around my neck, and whispers, "That was fun, Mommy," and falls asleep. And my heart grew three sizes that day. And somehow I knew that, even in my wrong way, I had done the right thing—that years down the road I wouldn't remember the lost hours of work. I would remember him laughing and running in his bare feet. Before he stubbed his toe on that rock.

You probably don't have a toddler. You probably don't work from home. But just like me, you probably miss some of the precious, spontaneous opportunities to jump up and go blow some bubbles. Let's don't do that anymore. Okay?

P.S. Who decided a thirty-seven-piece multifaceted, battery-operated, monogrammed bubble set with retractable pieces and a matching keychain should be fifty-nine cents at Target, but toilet paper costs me four dollars? I guess the same people who decided to charge us for air at the gas station.

- Anything worth having takes work

- There is no quick fix

- There is no fast answer

Discussion Questions:

1. Are you trying to put scotch tape on a busted water pipe? Are you looking for a quick answer? Maybe the answer won't come in one step. Why not just take it one step at a time?

2. What are the things in your life that you are most proud of? What did you have to do to get or achieve them?

Myth #15 SUPERHERO GETS CLOBBERED AND WALKS AWAY

Sometimes to win the battle you've got to get wounded

Wouldn't it be nice if we could have a boulder dropped on us from an overpass that flattens us, and yet we bounce back up and keep going? My mother is like that. Her arm can be severed at the elbow and she'll say, "Oh, it's okay. I'm fine. Just a little flesh wound. Let me just slice this roast with my good hand."

Somewhere along the way we got this idea that when we get clobbered we're supposed to keep going—shake it off—that it's weak to need to admit you need a nap, or some help, or a paramedic. I have a friend whose father knew he was having a heart attack and didn't want to bother anybody, so he drove himself to the doctor and waited patiently in the lobby until they could fit him in. Way I see it, you don't get points for being a superhero these days. They'll just call you stupid.

If you don't take a break, nobody will give it to you. And you're no good to anybody else if you're running on empty. Sometimes life can clobber you pretty good. It's okay if you want to shut yourself in your room, eat a box of chocolates in your tattered bathrobe, and sing with Aretha about how you get no respect. And sometimes your wounds can't be healed with chocolate and soul music, and you need to have the courage to ask for help. I had a good friend who was worried that if she asked for the help she so desperately needed, it would mean she couldn't do it on her own and that she was a bad mom. When the truth of the matter was that what would make her a bad mom was not asking for help when she needed it.

- Sometimes we get clobbered and need to stop and rest

- Know when you need to ask for help

- Asking for help is a sign of strength, not of weakness

Discussion Questions:

1. Do you have scheduled times that are just for you—when you can rest and refill your tank?

2. Sometimes it's as easy as taking an hour a day that's yours and yours alone. Why not find a time and set a goal of devoting that time to yourself? Share with others how you give back to yourself in the busyness of life.

3. Are you afraid to admit when you need help? Would you rather do it all yourself than ask someone else to do it? Do

you slam things around wishing other people would offer to help rather than just ask them?

Myth #16 LIFE IS SIMPLE

Hello Internet

It took me a while to figure out what was missing from those fairy tales—why it felt so, well, *quiet.* Then it occurred to me. The princess doesn't have a cell phone growing out her ear. She isn't texting her friends every thirty seconds. She doesn't have two hundred show tunes on her iPod. She doesn't have to stop on her way to take a basket of bread to her sick grandmother to post her new pictures on her MySpace page. She doesn't have to sift through a hundred spam emails or field calls from strangers in Budapest who don't want to sell her anything, they just want to conduct a short survey. She doesn't have six calls to return, a stack of bills to pay, or fifteen clocks to set because the time changed again. And she didn't have that blasted Bluetooth.

"I'm excited about your birthday present," my husband said to me, holding up a small FedEx package with a bow attached, wearing the same expression as last year when he handed me my new gutter irrigation system. "It's something you can use," he said, "to make your life easier." No way could that package hold an overweight Russian nanny named Svetlana who loves taking the kids to Chuck E. Cheese and cleaning toilets. I wasn't buying it.

"It's a Bluetooth!" he exclaimed, as I stared at this odd little black device that looked like a plastic roach. "You put it on your ear. It's so you can talk on your cell phone without using your hands!" His face flushed in excitement. "This way you can carry the groceries while you talk!" What a kind man—to be so concerned with my welfare. I knew he was still mad at having to fish my cell phone out of the toilet. I'm not technologically savvy, but I must admit that the idea of being able to make calls without using my hands was appealing. Even if he did have to spend an hour explaining how it worked.

"Does it play music?" I asked, turning it over.

"No, sweetie, you can't download music on it," he said with a condescending smile.

"What about TV channels? Will it get *American Idol?*"

"No, you can't get *American Idol.* It's a phone." He gritted his teeth.

"What about GPS, like in the commercial? Can it give me directions in my ear? That would be really cool."

He looked at me like he didn't recognize me and spoke really slow. "It's Bluetooth. You use it to talk on the phone without using your hands. That's it."

"Oh."

It was weird at first, having this device in my ear. It didn't look right with my hair or any of my outfits. And it was so light that I'd accidentally brush against it, and once I thought it was a roach and swore I felt it move, and I screamed and almost ran the car into a homeless guy. But somewhere along the way I started to enjoy the benefits of modern technology. I liked the looks I would get from people who figured I must be somebody important. I began to wear it everywhere: the drugstore, the doctor's office, the gas station. Suddenly I couldn't wait for the phone to ring so that I could now do sixteen things at once, instead of the mere fourteen I was limited to before owning this life-saving device.

Three days I wore that thing and not one call, except for the telemarketer who has now removed me from his calling list because I kept him on the phone for thirty minutes while I tested all the features. "Okay, now let me call you this time and practice putting you on hold. If we disconnect, call me back. And I still want to try this button to the right. Ooh, here's the volume. Now this is cool. Can you call me again and this time put me on hold? What about Fred in the cubicle beside you? Can we bring him on again? Okay, can you hear me now? Get it? Hear me now? That is you guys, isn't it?"

Now I understand what all those people were doing: talking to themselves in cars with both hands still on the wheel; chatting at empty walls in airports. The cute guy I thought was hitting on me and the lady I chatted with all the way from auto parts to cat litter. No wonder she kept giving me weird looks. I thought those people were a little touched and added them to my prayer list. But they weren't crazy, except for the old lady tasting the detergents—pretty sure she was the exception. Now that I owned a Bluetooth, I worried that people would think I was talking to myself, until I realized I talked to myself before I owned Bluetooth, so this device would actually give me more credibility. I finally had an excuse. Ninety percent of the time I talked, the thing wasn't even turned on.

I try to be a polite Bluetooth user, but I have an annoying habit of yelling when I talk on my Bluetooth. I can't explain it, but something about that device makes me think anyone who calls me is deaf. Turns out my Bluetooth is voice-activated to recognize verbal commands, which I also feel compelled to yell. My Bluetooth and I have a love-hate relationship. When we're good, we're really good. When we're bad, it's not pretty.

I was so excited about the voice activation feature that I spent the entire first day yelling commands: CALL MOM—CALL BILL AT WORK—CALL THE POST OFFICE—CALL VOICE MAIL. I would get distracted, and while waiting for change at McDonald's yell, "CALL HOME" to the complexion-challenged redhead who was still mad at me for yelling "CALL 911." At first it was cool to talk to my Bluetooth, with the exception of that little incident where I was so busy talking I knocked over a display rack of pantyhose. Yeah, it was fun at first. Not so much anymore. Mainly, because I am from the South and apparently my Bluetooth isn't. We seem to have a verbal disconnect. I think she—yes, she—gets mad because I yell and call my voice mail every hour for no other reason than just to play with the device. And I think every so often she gets into a bad mood and just wants to remind me who's in charge.

"CALL HOME PLEASE," I yell, deciding to check my messages for the third time in an hour. Oops. Not turned on. Okay, let's try again. Bleep. "Please enter your command," she says for the fourth time that day. I swear I heard her sigh.

"CALL HOME PLEASE," I yell, a little louder this time.

"Did you say, call police?" she asks sweetly.

"NO, I SAID CALL HOME PLEASE!"

"Did you say, call Belize?"

"NO! HOME. CALL HOME!"

"Did you say, call Shalom?" she asks.

"NO! AND WHO WOULD YOU CALL ANYWAY? WHO IS SHALOME? I SAID CALL HOME. H-O-M-E—HOME. CALL HOME!"

"Did you say, call Rome?" she asks.

"NO! I DIDN'T SAY CALL ROME. I SAID CALL HOME!"

"Calling Rome, please wait," she says. I swear she's smirking. I hang up, debating whether or not to try it again. Yes. It is now a matter of principle.

Bleep. "Please enter your command," she says for the fifth time that day.

"Call home," I say in my best northern accent, trying to disguise my voice.

"I'm sorry. Could you repeat your command?"

"OH FORGET IT! I'LL JUST DIAL THE STUPID NUMBER MYSELF!"

"About time," she whispers.

Thank you, dear hubby, for my new toy. I thought road rage was my anger threshold. Nice to see that the bar has now been raised. Thank you for the gift intended to make my life easier.

P.S. For the record, your calls are not free when you use your Bluetooth, especially during something called "peak hours." My husband says he'll explain it to me when he calms down.

Technology is great, no doubt about it. But do we need to be available everywhere we go? Email is great, but do we need to spend hours sorting through the messages and getting up in the middle of the night because we thought we heard the soft ding of an incoming message? Computers are great, but do we need to be a slave to them? Technology is supposed to make your life easier, not harder. Put it back in its place.

- Let technology be your tool, not your master

Discussion Questions:

1. Calculate how much time you spend answering emails. Do you set aside a specific time of day to answer emails or are you checking them all day long? Consider having designated times to answer emails. If you work from home, choose one time for emails that need to be answered during business hours, and save the rest for the off-hours that aren't better spent generating business.

2. Are you available to people wherever you go? Is it necessary? Must you be reached at every moment? Schedule some times when you turn off the phones.

3. Would the world end if you disconnected your answering machine for a while? I know—it sounds crazy. But think

about it. They know they need to call back and you have a day of peace and quiet.

4. Make sure your email has a good spam filter so you don't spend unnecessary time filtering those messages out.

Myth #17 HEROES ARE ONLY IN BOOKS

That depends on how you define heroes

If you've ever been an active participant in a toddler's potty-training season, you know the tremendous victory when he finally conquers his fears and, without prompting, deposits his first unsolicited stinky in the potty. I still remember the day my son finally crossed the finish line. There were hoorays, high fives, and tears of relief that my son won't be the only kid on the football team wearing a pull-up. I kissed him, gave him the five-pound bag of candy I had promised, and put a nice cap on what was already a treasured moment by promising him a trip to the auto shop—his favorite place in the whole world. Forget *Disney on Ice,* forget Elmo at the coliseum—take my kid to watch Buster breathe life into a Dodge Duster and my kid hits toddler nirvana. Unfortunately, this is never as cheap a form of entertainment as I would hope. It is the auto shop after all.

My son starts shaking in excitement at the mere sight of that giant plastic tire in the sky and we pull into one of those quaint small-town operations, where not only can you get your tires rotated while Hank sings his sorrows from the dusty old radio, you can find out whose kid is sure to be crowned homecoming queen, hear where old man Jenkins turned up this week on his wayward scooter, and even buy some bait if you feel so inclined. All to the sounds of various auto shop tools that form the symphony my son so loves. I'm convinced that when his Sunday school teacher sings about heaven, this is what he sees.

I am still getting out of the car when my son bolts out of the back seat and sprints across the parking lot so fast I feared the wind would catch hold of his protruding ears. He is partly fueled by the candy that has left a perfect O-shaped chocolate ring around his mouth, and partly fueled by the fact that he has got news to share. Big news. And before I have time to stop him, he comes to a screeching halt in front of the row of open garage doors, takes a deep breath, and screams in his loudest voice to date, "I went stinky on the potty!" My heart stopped from extreme embarrassment and time stood still, as his announcement echoed and bounced through the walls of the auto shop and down Main Street, where they stopped pumping gas three blocks down. I debated the idea of pretending I'd never seen this kid and making a run for it, but I figured that might turn around and bite me. So I just smiled the same "what can you do?" smile I pasted on when he sang "Jesus Loves Me" down every single aisle of the grocery store.

What felt like an eternity in that parking lot was really, in retrospect, only a second when he screamed, "I went stinky on the potty," and without hesitation there came from the bays in that garage a unifying, resounding male cheer from under cars and behind hoods. It was no less enthusiastic than had he just scored the game-winning touchdown in the Super Bowl. "Way to go," they cried. "Good job," they screamed, as the air filled with waving wrenches and power drills. And my son beamed as his greatest heroes in the whole world stopped what they were doing to recognize his accomplishment. And in that moment, they became my heroes too.

Don't be so quick to assume that there are no heroes. They are everywhere. You just have to look for them. They aren't always the ones wearing the capes.

- Real-life heroes exist—you just have to look a little closer to find them

Discussion Question:

Think about the people in your life who are heroes and why. Think about who may be looking at you as a hero.

Myth #18   THE ONE WITH THE MOST CASTLES WINS

More stuff will not make you happy

I'm a sucker for any kitchen gadget sold on TV. Show me a woman in a dated hairdo and a pantsuit, waving her hand over a seventy-five-piece plastic monogrammed food-packaging and storage system, and my pulse starts to race. Show me the whole family frolicking (is that still a word?) through the meadow with the dog and the handy-dandy monogrammed food-packaging carrying case on wheels with the drink holder and solar radio, and I'm diving for my credit card. Tell me that for just an additional dollar, I can get a complete set of stainless steel knives guaranteed to cut steel and to outlive three generations, and it is no longer a want, no longer a need—it has become *I must have this or I will die.* Forget braces for Junior; Mamma needs a food storage system.

My husband tried to block the channel after I ordered him thirty-seven Button-Me-Easy kits that promise to replace your button in thirty seconds without the need for needles or thread. He said it would have been a good idea, if his shirts had buttons.

It happens again yesterday. Just when I've barely recovered from the ramifications of ordering a lifetime supply of under-the-bed sweater organizers that emit a lilac scent, I see her white teeth and that familiar pantsuit, and I'm under her spell again. This time is different. This gadget is the king daddy of all gadgets: the Air Sucker 2000, breaking all records in high-tech kitchen gadgetry. Put your food in the bag, slide the bag through the sealer, and it sucks all the air out of the bag and keeps it fresh for the rest of your life—just as fresh as the day you put it in. We're thinking of using it on Great Uncle Fred. You can seal pork chops, chicken, steak, salad, soup, and even a pint of your dog's blood should he ever need a transfusion. This would have been a handy thing to have when Uncle Skeeter cut off his toe with the weed whacker and we needed something to carry it in.

This is revolutionary. This will save us millions of dollars in wasted food. *This* I have to have. I decide to order three—just in case they stop making them.

"What are you doing?" my husband asks in an accusing tone as I'm reciting my credit card number to Susie, who swears the Air Sucker 2000 kept her from losing her husband. How does he do that? I have to yell for help *four* times when I super-glue my foot into my new shoe (long story). It takes ten minutes for him to come to my aid when I get my hair caught in the drain (even longer story). We have a dead squirrel on the front porch for three days and he doesn't even notice. Pick up the phone to try and place a tiny little credit card order and it's like I blew a dog whistle.

I tell Susie to please hold, roll my eyes, and explain to my husband, while trying to be patient, that this is one of those necessary purchases. "You do NOT need that," he says, gritting his teeth. He should really learn to handle stress more effectively.

"Yes, I do."

"Like you needed the battery-operated Bug-Be-Gone for the pool?" He can be quite sarcastic when he wants to be.

"Hey, you said yourself that was good idea," I point out.

"We don't have a pool!" he growls. I hang up the phone before Susie can call 911 to report domestic violence, and follow my husband to the kitchen, where he's standing with his arms crossed, wearing that look he gets when he's about to win an argument. Uh-oh.

"Open that cabinet," he barks. "Come on. Open it. And tell me what you see." I don't appreciate his tone.

"Let's see," I murmur. "There's the green-pepper spiraler...the vegetable blender with the pasta attachment...the six-speed juicer with the sleeve to hold the morning paper...oh, here's that cute serving tray with the ceramic pigs in bikinis on pool floats...and the pasta colander that turns into a centerpiece...and I'm not really sure exactly what this thing is..." My voice trails off as I crawl deeper into the cabinet.

"What's that behind the silver-plated cake stand that sings happy birthday?" he asks, while I drag out a dust-covered contraption and read the words on the side: AIR SUCKER 2000. Suddenly it comes rushing back: November, two years ago. I still remember the day it came in the mail. I was so excited. I was convinced that this revolutionary item would change my life. I never could figure out how it worked. It was missing three pieces, wouldn't work on any speed but high, made an awful screeching noise, blew a fuse, and was wider than my counter top. I wrapped one piece of chicken (which is still in my freezer, thank you very much) and decided it wasn't worth the effort.

Okay, okay, so maybe my husband has a point. He's still a little mad. It's probably better that I don't tell him there are three more Air Suckers in the basement.

I think one of the reasons that so many of us women like to shop is that we truly think more stuff will make us happy—one more pair of shoes, one more pair of black pants, one more candle, one more battery-operated cell phone charger, just in case. When will enough be enough? When will we be content with what we have? As long as they don't come out with the Air Sucker 3000.

- More stuff will not make you happy, so put down that pair of shoes

Discussion Questions:

1. Is there anything in the closet with a price tag still on it? Anything older than one week?

2. Do you find yourself saying once a day, "I need to go get..."

3. Do you see something and have to have it?

4. Do you wish you could stop buying, buy anyway, and then feel guilty about it and swear you won't do it again?

5. Think back to last year—to something you bought that you just had to have. Was it as important as you thought it was?

Myth #19   WE'RE ALL AFRAID OF THE BIG BAD WOLF

Even though we've never seen him

I never used to get scared when I was young, single, and living in an apartment complex overlooking the projects where even the sound of gunfire didn't keep us from opening a ground floor window to catch a breeze. I felt safe surrounded by my family of strangers, who made window art out of beer cans, whose cars vibrated to the beat of their own drums, and who were prone to pack up and move in the middle of the night. I slept soundly to the pulse of the blue light blinking through my bedroom window. But somewhere between marriage, motherhood, and moving into a quiet house in a nothing-out-of-the-ordinary neighborhood, I became a chicken. Suddenly I'm convinced that it has become the American burglar's dream to get his hands on our dusty VCR, hand-me-down televisions, wallet with three dollars and a handful of Chuck-E.-Cheese tokens, and a collection of Beanie Babies that I am convinced will get us through retirement. Or even worse, to have his way with me, which even I have to admit makes for a pretty desperate burglar.

I considered an alarm system, but decided that I would rather be taken by surprise and killed than hear an electronic voice whisper from my bedroom wall that an intruder is coming up the stairs. In fact, I would probably take myself out just to spare myself the agony of suspense. And with my luck, I would get the electronic alarm voice with the bitter just-left-my-husband attitude: "See, I told you he was breaking in, you fool. Next time maybe you'll listen to me. I'm thinking you asked for that one. You should never have gotten married; this fool here isn't going to protect you. That's a man for you." No, I didn't need an alarm system. I married an ex-football-playing power lifter who is convinced that he can kill someone with his bare hands, despite the fact that our living-room bookshelf collapsed in the middle of the night last week and he didn't even wake up. I've pretty much resigned myself to the fact that if the burglar wants to come in, there's nothing that can stop him. I think the makers of alarm systems need to talk to the makers of toy packaging. If burglars had to work as hard getting into a house as parents have to work to open a new toy—the hard plastic, those twist ties, all those tiny screws—that boogey man will not stay the course. I'm just saying.

It's when hubby goes out of town that I struggle. I'm not scared at the thought of him going, and certainly not scared enough that I can't plan an enjoyable evening of scallion chicken, chocolate, scented candles, *Gray's Anatomy*, three episodes of *Law and Order*, and a *Lifetime* movie about a woman being stalked by her lover's ex-girlfriend's crazy roommate, starring Judith Light. For some weird reason I'm not scared earlier that afternoon, or at dinner, or at 9:00 P.M., or at 10:00 P.M., or even at 11:00 P.M. But at 11:01 my eyes start to shift and campy horror-music tracks start running through my head. In my mind, that's when the boogey man clocks in and starts creeping slowly down the street in his rusty old Dodge Dart with a trunk full of duct tape and Hefty bags. I am not scared until I put on my fuzzy socks and flannel nightgown (just so he won't be tempted), and crawl under the covers. That's when I hear the noise. Never fails. Every time, I hear a noise. I do a quick run-through of all the explainable noises: ice maker, cat, air conditioner, leaky faucet, sound of the whistle inside my own nose. None of these. I am convinced that this is a noise only the boogey man can make.

I try to be logical—what are the odds that this guy would choose my house?—which doesn't make me feel any better, because it's the same logic I used when I convinced myself nobody would see me if I ran out to the mailbox in my leotard. That story didn't end well. There are still children in therapy over that one. In fact, odds were good that he was going to pick my house, because I had just mopped the floors and wouldn't that just be a kicker: to go out after having spent hours cleaning your floors—like washing your car and it rains. Those are my kind of odds. Okay, so I didn't actually mop them, I swept them. Okay, okay, so I just used the dust buster in the corners—what are you, the clean police? I considered making the boogey man's job easier by going ahead and putting all my belongings on the front porch so he wouldn't have to come in. But my lazy side convinced my fearful side that was a bad idea. Besides, last time I left piles of stuff on the curb, even the bums rejected it. I considered sleeping in a different room to surprise him, but that would mean having to wash the sheets in the guest bedroom.

I imagine the boogey man looking through my car, trying to remove the expensive electronic equipment that's not there, and I can actually hear him swear as his fingers wrap around a petrified French fry and the chewed-up nugget remains that have grown hair in between the seats. I see his lips curl up in disgust as he flips through my CD collection. If he were a smart burglar, he'd go for the bag of diet bars in the back seat that cost more than my car is now worth. Shoot, if he were smart, he'd pick a different house. Take the CDs, by golly, but those diet bars cost me a fortune. Only in America does it cost more money to eat less.

Great, now he's mad and he's coming inside. I know this because I can hear him picking the lock downstairs. So what if I can't hear my husband when he gets locked out and bangs for thirty minutes on the front door? Now I am sure I can hear that boogey man breathing and breaking into the house in slow motion, because that's what they do, you know—move in slow motion while looking both ways like kids about to cross the street. So much for the big dog house that's supposed to scare him away. I'm convinced that he's been casing the house long enough to know that the scary big dog went to the vet and didn't come home, whereupon the burglar hotline went crazy: "Dog gone at the Swansons. I repeat: Dog gone at the Swansons."

That's when I realize I don't have the phone: Dummy, any fool knows that you won't have time to get the phone if it's across the room. But now I'm worried. Do I have time to get to the phone before he reaches the top of the stairs? Should this time be better spent finding a hiding place? And would I still fit on the top shelf of my closet like I imagined when I was smaller? Should this time be spent trying to get out of the bathroom window—oops—the same window that won't open anymore because I painted over it by mistake? Great. I can hear my husband now, leaning over my dead body, saying, "Well, you might have gotten away if you had listened to my advice. That's what you get when you do a rush job." I decided to make a run for the phone. I'm still here, so obviously it was a good call. Excuse the pun. Even when I'm scared, I've still got it.

Then I can hear the sound of his pickax brushing the wall, going up the stairs. It's weird how your heart can be throbbing through your chest, your life can be flashing before your eyes, you can be picking out thirty-seven escape routes and hiding places, and still wonder if this is the night gown you should be caught dead in, picturing your blue-haired relatives leaning over the casket saying, "What a shame. So young. You think she could have picked a better gown. I didn't realize she had put on that much weight."

These are the times when I always wish I had taken a self-defense class. I try to remember everything my husband told me to do when you're getting attacked. Shove him up the nose. No, too gross. Poke him in the eyes. Eeeewwww, even worse. No way. Knee him in the groin, maybe, but last time I tried to hike my knee up in aerobics I fell down. "Beat him until he doesn't get up," my husband tells me, "over and over." He obviously didn't see me when I cried in kickboxing class because my knuckles got scraped. He obviously hasn't seen my bruises from trying to get my four-year-old dressed. My husband has this image of me that doesn't exist, perhaps never did. He didn't know me the time I ran into the cement pole in front of Family Deal Barn because I was looking down at my shoes to see if they made my feet look big. He didn't see me wave and smile at the swaying drunk guy who was peeing on the dumpster outside the Gas 'n Go because I didn't want him to think I was rude. The idea of me overwhelming my attacker is about as realistic as the idea of me passing a donut shop without stopping.

It is for these reasons that I consider myself a pacifist, but sometimes the mind does crazy things and I decide that in order to protect myself and my sleeping child, it's time to get the gun. Yes, I said it. We have a gun. Not my idea. My husband brought guns into the marriage. I do not like guns, and the idea of giving one to me is like giving a knife to someone with seizures—you don't know what will happen but you can bet it won't be good. But drastic times call for drastic measures, and the gun is closer than the knives in the kitchen. I can somehow imagine myself shooting someone from a distance easier than trying to knife him the same way I poke a potato. I am sweating just thinking about the gun which is hidden in the top shelf of a closet in the next room. There are no bullets in it, so the best I can hope for is to throw it at him. But sitting there wide-eyed in my granny nightgown at 3:00 A.M.—well, I'm not thinking clearly. I go for the gun. I practice pointing and saying, "Make my day. This is going to hurt me worse than it hurts you. I have a gun and I'm not afraid to use it. Give me all your axes." Okay, so at least I was entertained and momentarily forgot my fear. Until I had to pee.

Everybody knows that there are two moments when the traditional boogey man will strike: when you're in the shower and when you're squatting—both very vulnerable positions. Not as vulnerable though as if it were the middle of your annual female exam. That would never happen though, because the boogey man would take one look at the stirrups and syringes and run. Or tell him the stick turned pink and that'll get rid of him. I should sleep at the doctor's office when hubby is out of town—kind of like hunkering down in a safe bunker, or whatever the expression is.

Anyway, the movies never show you how to handle the whole having-to-pee situation. But now I really have to go. Surely I can't put the gun down, or he'll grab it and turn it on me—or rather throw it at me, as the case may be. There is only one choice. I have to pee and stay armed at the same time. I once drove three miles, in the rain, with broken wipers, while applying lipstick and changing a diaper. I can do this. And I do. And with great skill and manual dexterity, might I add. I complete my business and never once take my finger off the trigger. Annie Oakley, you got nothing on me.

Now I'm back in the bed, eyes wide, brandishing the gun wildly around the room and realize that my child is sleeping across the hall, and what if the boogey man goes there first? Although there are days when I am convinced that if my wild-eyed toddler ever got abducted, they would certainly bring him back, I just don't want to take any chances. And it's usually at this point that I run into his room and grab him, and bring his snoring body back to my bed where I am fully prepared to throw myself over him and yell, "Take me! Take me!" But now I've got the sleeping kid and the gun, and I don't want him to wake up and see the gun—bullets or not. And what if my husband comes home early for some reason and can't reach me on the phone that is lying on my stomach because the battery has suddenly gone dead, and so I don't know he's coming, and he sneaks in and I don't hear him and I shoot him by mistake—and I know there are no bullets in there, but good grief, how can you be sure? I'm certainly not going to open it to find out.

I decide that I would rather be shot than accidentally shoot my family, and I put the gun under the bed. Nope, not a good idea, because undoubtedly Junior will pull it out, covered in dust bunnies the size of a small dog—he finds everything—and he'll start playing with it and put it in his backpack (despite the fact that he still can't work the zipper), take it to school, and he'll get expelled from preschool and I'll get arrested, and they'll say this is why the world is in the state it's in—she was the mom who sent chocolate bars for snack instead of carrots. And I'll go to jail and end up rooming with a boogey man or boogey lady, as the case may be, and find out that it was her cousin who broke into my house and caught me on the john and still has the mental scars to prove it. Better to put it back on the top shelf of the closet and resort to plan B, where I tell the criminal to please hold a minute while I run and grab my unloaded gun.

It is 4:30 A.M. and I'm wide awake, with one arm on the phone, fingers gripping my new razor in the hopes of nicking him to death, and the other arm on my Bible, having decided my best chance at scaring him off would be to witness to him (he would either run or be saved, either of which would work in my favor), while my son snores loudly beside me. And then somehow—as I'm praying that if this is my night to die, to please make sure that my husband does not find anyone else skinnier, and if there could be chocolate in heaven I would be really happy—by some wonderful miracle, I fall asleep and wake up at that magical hour of 6:00 A.M., where I am no longer afraid because the sun is now coming up and everybody knows that the boogey man gets off work at 6:00 A.M., just like he gets snow days and Christmas Eve off. And I drift back to sleep and all is right with the world and there is peace. I have had my brush with death and lived to write about it. Little do I know that there is another fear lurking just around the corner (when I would mistakenly think that with just a little bit of spandex I could fit my size fourteen body into a size ten pair of jeans. I still have the bruises to show for it).

P.S. Did you know the average burglar only makes $4,000 a year? What if that's based on just one good hit? That's not bad if you average it. I think he's making more than I am.

All this to say, that there are many things out there for us to be afraid of—so why worry about the things that haven't happened yet? Today has enough troubles of its own. Worry about tomorrow tomorrow. Don't spend your life looking for the boogey man.

- Don't worry about things that haven't happened yet

- Focus on today, for today has enough troubles of its own

- Walk yourself through the worst-case scenario—then you've faced the worst that can happen and realized that you can get through it

Discussion Questions:

1. What do you spend your time worrying about? Do you worry about things that probably won't happen? Do you lay awake at night asking yourself questions that start with *what if?*

2. Out of all your worries, what is affecting you today? What needs to be handled right now? And what can wait?

3. What are you afraid will happen? Can you stop it? Can you fix it? Can you control it? Have you exhausted all options? Then let it go. Let the worst happen and you just might find that it wasn't as bad as it could have been.

Myth #20 IT'S NOT FUNNY

Maybe not, but laugh anyway

It was another quiet day at the Fix 'N Stitch Medical Center when they got word that a bus full of senior citizens had run into a chicken truck up Route 29. This was big news to a small town whose last major excitement occurred when Harvey swallowed his hearing aid at the potluck supper. Edsel, who was driving, did not have time to dodge the chicken truck or the lone chicken that hit the windshield first, in what some are now calling a suicide mission. And that's how the chicken truck ran into the senior citizen bus up Route 29, causing a commotion that would have caused traffic to back up for miles, if they had traffic to begin with.

Ernestine Finglebottom, who was sitting on her front porch writing in her diary when she witnessed the whole thing, said there was a horrendous screeching of tires, clashing of metal, and great gnashing of teeth, whereupon chicken feathers blanketed the scene in what she titled in that day's diary entry: *Poultry in Motion.* We questioned her on the "gnashing of teeth" part and she admitted that she wasn't sure what that meant, but she'd been waiting for years to use it. Ernestine was a self-appointed wordsmith with a vivid imagination, considering that at the time of said accident both vehicles were traveling at the speed of my Great Aunt Lilly pushing her walker through the drugstore. Nobody was seriously hurt, but the victims did not know this yet and were taking full advantage of this opportunity to panic. They were low on ambulances, so they borrowed some hearses from the funeral home next door. You can imagine the victims' distress when they saw the line of somber hearses coming up over the hill, and they started looking for pearly gates and placing bets as to which side of the proverbial line they would fall.

The double doors of the medical center opened, and the screeching sound of gurneys announced the end to the quiet afternoon and the beginning of what could only be described as chaos dressed in blue hair and orthopedic shoes. "All hands on deck! I repeat! All hands on deck!" Barb screamed, amid the sea of wandering cardigans and disoriented chickens. Barb, head nurse, thrived on drama. She was only working at the medical center until she finished her online real estate course: a fifty-seven-piece box set that guarantees upon completion you'll make over 100,000 dollars a month. We all agreed it showed more potential than her last project— producing her own exercise video. We were still shuddering at the image of Barb in a thong leotard and leg warmers yelling, "Crunch those buttocks. Crunch those buttocks!"

Getting them all to their rooms was like herding cats, which happened to be Barb's forte, as two years prior she was an integral part in creating the first-ever feline circus, Paws for Applause, which unfortunately had fatal results with lawsuits still pending.

"Am I dead? Is this heaven? Just tell me! Am I dead?" Harvey yelled as Bert tucked in his sheets.

"No, Harvey, you are not dead," Bert said. "And this is not heaven. See? Rectal thermometer is still here." Harvey's roommate Ethel broke out into a passionate rendition of "Are You Washed in the Blood?" in a shrill voice that was a full octave higher than dolphins and had caused a handful of dogs to gather outside the window. Harvey stared at her in disbelief, grabbed Bert's hand, and whispered, "Kill me now! Just kill me now!"

Flora Joy wouldn't take her pain medication because she was convinced it was a conspiracy to turn her brain to mush so men could have their way with her, like she saw on that women's channel. Pity on the soul who would resort to having his way with Flora Joy—a woman whose mission in life was to bring facial hair back in style. Betty McAllister was upset because in all the chaos her lips had made contact with a chicken beak, and now she was convinced that she had that dreaded bird flu and, come to mention it, her lips were feeling a bit numb. But she didn't want any of that conspiracy medication either, thank you very much—the last time she let a man have his way with her, he stayed for a month. Mrs. DeWitt kept yelling for room service because her sheets were a little scratchy, and could we please bring in one of those sweet little Vietnamese ladies to come do her nails. Loretta Cash was screaming for a piece of paper to write her last wishes, making it quite clear that she did not, and I repeat, did not, want anyone to pull the plug—by golly, she wanted to live. It soon became obvious she would be in the minority on that vote. Five minutes around that woman and people wanted to pull the plug. Please, let there be a plug.

Buster Tate, who was so inebriated they had to strap him into his bed, needed stitches—not from the accident, but from racing the gurneys down the hall. He took out two food carts, a ficus tree, and a feeble old lady before crashing into first place. The old lady was okay, but would forever need therapy to handle the flashbacks of Buster's hairy rear end smiling out from the slit in his gown like a monkey. We had no choice but to let May Belle do his stitches. May Belle was eighty-two, had been a candy striper for fifty-seven years, and had actually been laid off a decade ago, but nobody had the heart to tell her. Being an avid quilter, she was the backup plan when stitching was necessary, even though her sewing skills far outweighed her ability to see. But that didn't keep her from stitching her phone number across Booker's chest. May Belle was secretly looking for husband number three and could be unabashedly forward when it came to pursuing men.

The lobby soon filled with tearful relatives carrying casseroles and fighting over who would sing at Grandpa's funeral and who would get Granny's set of ceramic pig bookends, when she took off for that giant bingo table in the sky. And just when the chaos hit a crescendo, the clock struck four and the senior citizens froze in mid-sentence, looked at each other, and bolted, for nothing can light a spark under a group of well-meaning senior citizens like the call of the early bird special. The mother ship had called them home. And just like that, they were gone. And all was quiet again as the doors closed on the last patient and all that lingered behind was one chicken feather drifting to the ground like a streamer left behind after New Year's Eve. And they settled back into the tranquility of small-town living, every now and then stealing a longing glance out the window towards the horizon, wondering what would come next to break the spell.

Life is serious, yes. Which is why we should appreciate those random moments when humor makes an appearance.

- Appreciate that sometimes life is funny and it's okay to enjoy it

Discussion Question:

Recall a funny story and share it with others. Doesn't it feel good to laugh?

Myth #21   THE STORY ENDS AT THE LAST PAGE

It's never too late to rewrite your ending

"Read it again, Mommy, read it again," my son begs for the fourth time. He never grows tired of hearing it over and over and over. And he always wants to know what happens next.

"It's over," I tell him. "End of story."

But it's not like that in real life. Even when you're dead, it's not over. It's never too late to change, never too late to write a new chapter, never too late to run after a new dream. That's what Juggles did.

It was in January of 1962 when Barnsley P. Wentworth III told his father that he wasn't going to be a doctor; he was going to be a clown. Without hesitating, his father replied, "Then you will never amount to anything. Consider yourself a failure." That was the moment Barnsley P. Wentworth III fell from his father's grace, changed his name to Juggles, and became a clown. It was his greatest joy. It was his greatest passion. And he never made more than $50 a job.

It was a hot afternoon in July. Juggles was driving back to his hotel after working all day at a county fair, when he took a wrong turn into a trailer park and saw the mailbox covered in balloons—the calling card of a child's birthday party. He sat there for a moment, looked at his watch, shook his head, sighed, and grinned from ear to ear as he put his rubber nose back on and jumped out of the car. He saw a little red head peeking through the flowered sheet curtain, followed by piercing squeals as the door burst open and children rushed at him like excited puppies finding food. He would never forget that sound or the shocked look on the mother's face as she whispered "thank you" and started to believe again. Or the sheer adoration on the birthday boy's face as Juggles signed his cast, and he solemnly vowed never to wash his arm again as he hugged Juggles' striped leg, and that moment was branded into his memory as he whispered "thank you" and started to believe again.

Juggles never stopped being a clown. Day in and day out, it stayed his dream and remained his passion. Even when his hair fell out and he was too weak to honk his nose, even from his bed, when those few fans that were left had to come to him. It was March of 1998 when Juggles died, wearing a big red nose and a contented smile. He never made more than $50 a job.

How do you measure happiness?

- The book is not closed on your life
- It's never too late to change the ending or write a new chapter

Discussion Question:

What about you? Do you have another chapter left to write? Another dream to run after? Is it time to write a new ending? It's never too late.

ODE TO SPARKY

This one's just for fun

The vet said Sparky died of natural causes. Aunt Fern said it was probably something he ate. Mildred said that cat had been electrocuted, caught on fire, painted pink, and dressed up as a camel for the Buncam Baptist Christmas Pageant—that if that didn't add up to nine lives, nothing did. Personally, I think Sparky had finally had enough of this crazy family, got a hold of some pills, and took his own life. He just picked the wrong week to do it.

It was Great Uncle Edsel's ninetieth birthday and a great cause for celebration, since he wasn't supposed to live this long, having been diagnosed with some rare disease that none of us could pronounce. The doctors had given him a month, two at the most. We had accepted it, and so had Edsel, who had chosen to spend the remainder of his time intoxicated. That was ten years ago, and the man had soaked up so much alcohol we couldn't let him blow out the candles on his cake for fear he'd blow us all up. So nobody noticed

Sparky's suicide note, or discovered his contorted body, until the party was in full swing and the kids decided to play hide 'n seek. It was Sammy Junior who crawled under the bed to hide, and came eye to eye and cheek to cheek with the dearly departed Sparky, whose face had frozen in a wide-eyed snarl. It's safe to say that both of them were equally petrified. Sammy's scream circled the block as relatives ran in to face a situation far more interesting than hearing Uncle Bert's new country song, which had fourteen verses and ended up sounding like Hank Williams with a speech impediment. They all took turns peering under the bed and saying, "Yep, it's a dead cat all right." It was obvious that the next step was to remove Sparky from under the bed, and equally obvious that nobody wanted that job.

"You get it," someone whispered.

"I ain't touching it. You touch it!"

"I'm not touching it! You touch it!"

And the phrase was passed from one to another until they finally elected Big Ed, who was a cop. How much harder could this be than the time Old Man Foster passed out in the congealed salad at the little league picnic? Big Ed, with an image to protect, yelled for a broom, hitched up his pants, and bent down to survey the situation. Minutes later, with sweat-laced brow, he swept Sparky and a family of dust bunnies out from under the bed while we hovered behind him with held breath, staring at the cat who lay frozen on his back with all four paws up in the air, just like Aunt Ethel when she fainted during her solo at church because her girdle was too tight.

Somebody sneezed and Big Ed's arm jerked the broom and Sparky skidded across the floor, landing with a thud against Mildred's walker, creating instant hysteria as people literally climbed over each other to get out. It was a tragic moment that secured the job of every therapist within a thirty-mile radius. Mildred hyperventilated. Skeeter swallowed his snuff. And Aunt Bitsy says that was the trauma that caused her to start eating carbs again.

Once they got Uncle Edsel's heart started back up, they decided that they had no choice but to either bury Sparky or prop him up in a wing chair until the party was over. Loretta set off to find a box, because everybody knows the wing chair's reserved for Granny Jean once her medication kicks in. We tried getting Sparky into several boxes, but his tail kept popping out, causing shrieks of horror every time Ed tried to stuff it back in. Finally, we settled on little Emily's Barbie Camper with the side awning that made a great place for his tail. It was appropriate, as Sparky had always loved riding shotgun in Skeeter's mobile party camper with the flashing Budweiser light. The only place we could find dirt soft enough to dig was in the front yard.

So you can imagine the dismal scene we presented to the latecomers, who were now driving up to the party carting cases of beer, only to find us standing around a hole, with Big Ed digging knee-deep in dirt. We all paused, looked up, and Ed announced solemnly, "You're too late. He's already gone." The tardy relatives dropped to their knees, faces washed in grief (except for Vyrnetta, who showed no emotion at all, not from womanly grit, but the Botox injections she had received earlier that day). We found their reaction to be somewhat overdramatic until we realized they thought the hole was for Great Uncle Edsel.

We cleared up the confusion, showed them that Great Uncle Edsel was still alive, and let them get one last peek at Sparky. And except for that moment when Sparky's burial robe—a silver-sequined superhero cape with an S on the back—got caught on Erma's oxygen tank, the rest of the funeral went without a hitch. And that was the day dear old Sparky left this world. Great Uncle Edsel lived another ten years before deciding he'd had enough of this family too. We found him under the dining-room table. This time, thank God, he was dressed.

WHY MY COUSIN HAM BONE WON'T EAT SQUASH

Okay, just one more

Did I ever tell you why my cousin Ham Bone won't eat squash? Well, it all started on a Saturday morning, when Wade and Bo Junior were sitting on the front porch drinking Old Milwaukees, shooting cans off the dead tree stump, and listening to bugs fry in the zapper. Bo Junior was down in the dumps since his old girlfriend Erma Dean was getting married that morning down the street in her Aunt Eunice's back yard. So Bo Junior had the "don't know what you got till it's gone" blues and Wade was trying to cheer him up, which is why he thought it might be fun—and might get Bo's mind off of things—if they was to use that new tater gun they just made the other day, and drive by the wedding shooting spuds into the festivities. Needless to say, they were too young to have any real serious responsibilities, but old enough to know better than to engage in drive-by shootings of the potato persuasion. But sometimes Old Milwaukee does the thinking for you.

It wasn't hard for Wade to convince Bo Junior on the idea, as both of them had been itching to use that tater gun for something more productive than shooting Spidey the cat off the railing. Don't worry, it never hurt Spidey, just stunned him a little. When it came to backyard ballistics, Wade and Bo Junior had an unquenchable passion for coming up with bigger and better home-brewed devices for propelling weird objects through the air. I guess you could say it was their calling.

In case you aren't familiar with the intricate workings of spud gun artillery, it's the process of shooting potatoes out of pieces of pipe using various aerosol products as a propellant. Hence the name, "spud gun." For a little history of the spud gun, it evolved from the tennis ball gun of yesteryear, but now uses modern materials and construction techniques to provide a safer, more accurate, weapon system. PVC or ABS pipe, properly glued, provides a vastly superior barrel when compared to the soda-can/duct-tape structures of years ago.

Wade and Bo Junior decided to use hairspray as their propellant, being as Wade's cousin Juanita worked over at the five and dime and could get them a discount on cheap hairspray, resulting in a weapon that could shoot spuds nearly two hundred yards, thanks to the makers of Aqua Net. Later, thanks to Internet technology, Wade was to discover the beauty in the pneumatic spud gun, which used compressed air and could wreak havoc on enemy positions within a six-hundred-yard radius, and was the cause for their winning first place at the Pumpkin Chunkin' contest in Delaware, and the reason that now Bo Junior is missing his big toe. But at the time of this story, they were oblivious to such technological advancements, and so hairspray it was.

The plan was simple enough, and seemed harmless at its first construction. Sitting in the driveway to the side of the house, in the flat bed of a rusty, blue Ford pickup, sat a wire cage with a door on top, holding a flock of doves—or is it a pack, or a school? *What-ever.* The doves were waiting there, to be released at the end of the ceremony, which Wade and Bo Junior thought was downright stupid and deserved to be the target of their carefully aimed tater. Anyway, they were gonna pull the car up in front of the house, and Wade was gonna jump out and open the door to the cage so that the doves would fly out in one giant mass, and then Bo Junior was given the honors (thanks to his suffering heart) to direct the missile right into the middle of the pack, for no other reason than just to see what would happen.

It was probably what you would consider a dumb idea to begin with, but then they had to go and one-up themselves by attaching a string of firecrackers to the spud for a little added excitement. And they crept down the street in Bo's Mamma's old blue Buick, wearing baseball caps as disguises and trying to look inconspicuous as they aligned themselves into position.

Wade snuck out and unlatched the cage, then jumped back into the car, and Bo Junior took aim and fired. That spud sailed through the air at warp speed, beating even their own record for distance. Sailed right through the flock of doves with the sound of a baseball shooting through a ceiling fan, and the doves went hysterical, and that's when things started to go awry.

You see, the firecrackers never made it to their destination, coming dislodged upon being discharged from the gun, flying back into the Buick's back window and landing on top of Spidey, who had crawled into the back seat for a mid-morning nap. Let's just say that firecrackers and cats ain't a good combination, and Spidey took on supernatural powers and started ricocheting through that car like a popped balloon, landing directly on Wade's head, where he clung like he'd never clung before, which wasn't so good for Wade, who now looked like he was wearing a bushy hairpiece as he jumped out of the car screaming and running through the yard, straight into that wedding ceremony, looking like the ghost of Old Man Perkins, who met his untimely fate while coon hunting, when he stepped under the wrong tree and got attacked by the cousin of a coon he had snuffed on his last trip out. Clung to his head same as Wade's.

Needless to say, their getaway plan was foiled, and Bo Junior being the devoted friend he was, ran to Wade's rescue, trying to beat the cat off Wade's head with a plastic swan he found on his way in.

Meanwhile, the spud, after pegging the flock of doves, continued to whiz past the house to the back yard, where Erma Dean was now walking down the aisle towards her fiancé, Rick, singing Shania Twain's "From this Moment," in a high-pitched, screeching soprano that had to have been causing torment to every hound dog within a fifty-mile radius. Only her voice was drowned out by the screech of doves flying overhead, one of which had taken a plummeting detour directly into Porticia May Duberry's new hat, made special for that occasion and quite fitting to the theme, I might add, being as it was covered in plastic doves, which no doubt had been the cause of attraction for the real dove flying overhead, who must have taken on the heroic mission of saving that one plastic dove that he obviously had mistaken for a long-lost relative who'd gone missing about a year prior.

So you got the birds screeching overhead; the Lone Ranger dove flying into Porticia's hat, sending her into a fit of terror; Wade running through the ceremony with a cat clinging to his head; and that spud whizzing along its course of destruction. Needless to say, there was pandemonium.

Mildred Jenkins, as usual, thought it was the rapture, brought on by the blasphemy of singing Shania Twain at a holy ceremony, and she started screaming, "Take me now, Lord! Take me now!"

Meanwhile, Pastor Isaiah, who was officiating the ceremony, saw that tater flying through the air and, as fate would have it, he had had a dream just the night prior about his Great Aunt Ruth, who had choked on potato salad when he was a kid and died feet up, right in the middle of a family reunion, and his cousin Fern told him that Aunt Ruth was really a witch and would come back and haunt them one day, and whenever he'd see a potato he'd know she was nearby, and sure enough there was that spud with eyes just like Aunt Ruth's, and he passed out cold right there on the spot and fell over sideways, taking the daisy-lined arbor with him as he landed on top of three plastic swans.

Now Tater was the youngest groomsman in the wedding, being Erma Dean's cousin three times removed and once over. And Tater, in case you don't already know, has the most kid-envied, God-given gift of any boy in Cedar Grove, in that he can throw up at a moment's notice. Yep, all you got to do is say, "Tater, we need us a barf," and he'll have one halfway up his throat before you even finish your sentence. And in case you didn't know, Tater was one of John Henry's best friends, and John Henry was the town troublemaker. So it should be no surprise that John Henry (quite perturbed at having to miss his softball tournament to go to a stupid wedding) had coerced Tater into pulling up a last-minute barf at the conclusion of the ceremony, just to make things interesting—as if things weren't interesting enough at that wedding already. But anyway, Tater was all set to let loose a barf that day, having fully prepared by eating four helpings of his mamma's leftover squash casserole that day at lunch. And Tater's cue to unleash the hounds, so to speak, were the words "I do," which are a surefire part of any wedding ceremony, and certain to be the ideal moment for a prank of this nature.

Well, turns out that when Pastor Isaiah passed out after seeing the flying spud, and Hortence Duberry ran to his aid and started asking, did anyone know CPR, Enis Jones starts yelling from the back, "I do. I do." And Tater sets one off. But nobody can hear Enis over the chaos, and Hortence keeps screaming out, "Does anyone know CPR?" so that Enis keeps answering, "I do. I do," and Tater keeps setting off barfs in rapid succession, not one to miss a cue. Tater wasn't exactly what you'd call bright.

The groom's older brother, Bennie, had to join in the action and provide some assistance, being as he had skills in the life-saving department, having taken on a shift once at the volunteer fire department, and he leaned over to check the Pastor's pulse, and showed everyone firsthand why you shouldn't go without a belt, and that's how he come by the nickname "Buttcrack Bennie," and has been called that ever since.

So to recap, you got doves going crazy; Porticia wrestling with a dove of her own; Wade still trying to get the cat off his head while Bo Junior beats at it with a plastic swan; Pastor Isaiah passed out cold; Tater blowing chunks; Bennie baring his behind; and Erma Dean pitching a hissy fit at the sight of her perfect wedding being ruined in the middle of her heartfelt solo.

And that hairspray-propelled tater continues to hurl through the scene, ricochets off the pine tree, bounces off of the oak, whizzes through two blue-haired ladies, sails over Hershel—who, amazingly enough, managed to sleep through the whole thing thanks to a defective hearing aid—shoots underneath hand-crocheted wedding bells and begins its downward spiral, hits the water of the little manmade pond filled with floating magnolia candles, ending its journey by hitting dead-on one unsuspecting and unlucky catfish at exactly the right speed and magnitude to send it sailing through the air, whereupon it slaps Erma Dean upside the face before sliding down her wedding dress, where it frantically tried to wriggle its way to freedom. And as tight as that wedding dress was, honey, you could see every move it was making.

And Clayton (being the pervert that he is) dives in after it, horrifying Erma Dean's mother, who starts screaming that that filthy man is defiling the bride, to which the groom's mother shouts that someone's long since taken care of that. And Erma Dean's mamma cocked her head, let out an earth-shattering howl, and made a running lunge for the groom's mamma, catching hold of her hairpiece, which obviously was not securely attached, and the groom's mamma's hair goes flying through the air looking very much like a flying squirrel, which is what attracted Skeeter's hound dog Grunt, who had been dozing under the cake table, and he starts barking and chasing after it, jumping over chairs, and into old ladies' laps, tearing down streamer after streamer of plastic lilies. And the groom's mamma was so incensed at the loss of her new hairpiece that she took off her prosthetic leg and started beating Erma Dean's mamma with it. Still had the shoe on it and everything. And let me tell you, that woman could move around on one leg better than you probably would have given her credit for.

And then Big-Butted Bertha (no offense intended, as even her own family called her that) got into the scrapping match, 'cause even though she was just in town visiting her Granny Bee, and had been invited to the wedding out of sheer Southern politeness, she couldn't pass up the chance to partake in a good catfight. And for a while all you saw was Bertha living up to her nickname. I think it was that rear end that was the cause of two black eyes and a dislocated jaw.

And Clayton's girlfriend, all fired up after seeing her pervert of a boyfriend dive down headfirst into Erma Dean's cleavage, decides Clayton's about due for a whooping of his own, and she starts screaming at him, and flying at him with fists flying and fake fingernails flared, and opens a can of kick-butt on him that only went to prove there's a reason you should not wear a tube top to a wedding.

And it was at this exact moment that Myrlene's youngest boy, Frank Junior, the ring bearer in the ceremony, felt the call of nature, if you know what I mean, and had just learned to use the potty, but had also learned from his daddy that when you're outside, the same bathroom etiquette does not apply, and you can pretty much pick your spot—and he picked the water lilies attached to a nearby chair, figuring they could use some watering, to which the flower girl (Frankie Junior's cousin Noreen) screams in shock at the sight, to which the ring bearer turns in surprise, and is now watering the flower girl instead, who from what I hear is still in therapy to this day.

So to recap, you got wayward doves; Porticia wrestling with a dove of her own; Wade still trying to get the cat off his head while Bo Junior beats at it with a plastic swan; Pastor Isaiah passed out cold; Tater blowing chunks; Bennie baring his behind; Erma Dean with a fish set loose in her cleavage; the bride's mamma dodging the wooden leg; Big-Butted Bertha creating natural disasters right and left; Clayton getting ripped into by his girlfriend, who has now become the attraction of every pubescent boy within a fifty-mile radius; and Frank Junior answering the call of nature on his cousin Noreen.

And where's the groom in all of this? Standing there like an idiot, cheering for his mamma, the prosthetic-bearing warrior, much to the bride's dismay. Proving to her and everyone there that he was the spineless coward her friends had suspected him to be, and would never choose her over his own mother.

And it was right about now that Booker Diggs threw all caution to the wind and decided to crack open the six-pack he'd been saving for the post-wedding festivities, and he leaned back in his lounge chair, cracked open a cold one, and watched what had just turned into the most exciting wedding in history. He felt like he had a ringside seat at the boxing match. Why, there was so much going on, he didn't even know where to look, and whenever there was a lull in one place, he would resort to watching Great Aunt Clorice shaking her cane in the direction of the turmoil, trying to get a good whack in where she could, only she was fairly harmless being as her narcolepsy kept her from following through on most of her moves. And her sister, May Belle, was busy bending over the punch bowl, trying to fish out her teeth, which had fallen out while she was leaning over and filling her purse with petits fours and pigs in blankets to take home in case she got hungry later on. Yep, Booker almost became a believer that day, figuring only God could have worked things out this good. And suddenly he wasn't so perturbed at having to wear that scratchy, pale blue tux after all.

Meanwhile, Bo Junior finally gets the cat off Wade's head, and Spidey takes off in the direction of the chaos; Bo Junior takes off after her through all the commotion and trips over Booker's long feet, and falls flat at the feet of the woman who had broken his heart. Erma Dean. Love Muffin. The only woman he'd ever cared for enough to climb a water tower and paint her name. And as he was coming up on his knees, he realized that he loved her. Plain and simple.

And suddenly, Erma Dean's fiancé, Rick, takes notice of Bo Junior's entrance and decides all of the sudden that he's gonna be the big he-man and take charge of the situation and protect his woman, and he goes over and gets all up in Bo Junior's face, trying to act all brave I guess, 'cause Bo Junior was still trying to get to his feet. Well, this wasn't such a good idea, 'cause everybody knows that Rick wasn't no match for Bo Junior. And without even taking a breath, Bo Junior had him in a body lock, and wrestled him to the ground before Rick even knew what hit him, and pinned his neck down with his cowboy boot—a move he proudly borrowed from pro wrestling.

And Erma Dean looked down at her spineless groom and back at Bo Junior, and all these images come back of them holding hands at the monster truck rally. And how he'd broken her heart. Her Pookey-Poo. The only man she'd ever cared enough for to have his name airbrushed on her license plate. And she realized she loved him, plain and simple. And I'll be if this doesn't turn into a love story right before our very eyes.

And Bo Junior figured as long as he was already down on one knee anyway, he might as well propose. And he says, "Erma Dean, I'm sorry I told you your butt looked like two pigs wrestling under a blanket." And Erma Dean said, "Bo Junior, I'm sorry I told you you couldn't shoot the rear end of a buffalo if you were handcuffed to it." And Bo Junior said, "I never stopped loving you, Erma Dean. Will you marry me, baby?" And Erma Dean said, "Yes, I will." And they stood there kissing, and I must say, it was a heart-wrenching performance that would have brought tears to the eyes of the most cynical passerby.

And that very day, once the pastor was fully revived, Erma Dean and Bo Junior got married. And they've been married ever since. Yep, you don't hear love stories like that every day. And to think: It all started with a tater. Ain't it beautiful.

Ham Bone's the one told me that story to begin with. He was the groomsman standing beside Tater during the whole chunk-blowing episode, and privy to the amazing revelation that squash comes out exactly the same way as it goes down. Something most of us would probably be better off not knowing, including Ham Bone, who was never quite the same. And that is why Ham Bone to this day won't eat squash.

Back To Derk

Oh, yeah, back to Derk. So I go running out the door to claim my charming prince and live happily-ever-after. I didn't think it was odd that Derk was living in the basement of his mother's house, or that she would be sitting there beside us, knitting and chain-smoking cigarettes. I didn't think it was odd that Derk had gained fifty pounds and all the hair had slid off his head and landed on his back. I wasn't shallow—this was my Derk.

I didn't think it was weird that his room was still covered in trophies and pennants, or that he spent two hours telling me how he got his Corvette detailed. Or that the only time he asked about me was to ask if I'd kept up with the football team. And that he spent more time talking about what he was going to do than what he was actually doing. But when he yelled at me for sitting on his stuffed raccoon—okay, that was weird. And things got a lot weirder after that, especially when the dogs came into the picture.

I have nothing against dogs, but I do have something against a three-legged hound dog named Grunt who tries to do his business on my leg. And Derk's mamma yells out—without breaking the ash tip on her cigarette—that he's just marking his territory, and it would be in my best interest to keep moving, or Charlie, the Scottish terrier in heat, was going to land on me. And when they spent thirty minutes trying to get the poodle, Daisy, into her J-Lo birthday outfit—well, I could no longer hear them over the sounds of my fairy-tale characters screaming their way to a violent death. I don't think they even noticed that I snuck out while they were yelling at their afternoon soaps.

I drove around the neighborhood experiencing what I'll call a paradigm shift and a moment of silence for the Derk who was and is no more. That was when I finally accepted that life isn't a fairy tale and you don't always get what you wish for. Thank you, God.

Now I have a charming prince of my own, and I'm going to teach him that princesses aren't weak; that a prince can't ride up on a white horse and save everybody; that stepmothers aren't inherently evil; and that castles are hard to clean, not that I would know. And that life doesn't promise you a happily-ever-after. Or maybe it does—if you just know where to look.

Somewhere over the rainbow

Seems so far

'Til you find that the pot of gold

Sits right where you are

Then that over the rainbow

Fades away

Once you open your eyes and find

There's a whole new way

The Land of If Only

A little story
For those who are small
With a message
Big enough for us all

If you had wings
And could fly through the night
Up past the moon
And three stars to the right

If all were clear,
Look down and you'd see
The Land of If Only
Come, go there with me

In the Land of If Only
Grass is green, just like ours
Some days bring sun
And others bring showers

There are some who are short
And some who are tall
Some who have much
And some nothing at all

Look in that window
It's baker man Jake
Pounding the dough
For the bread that he makes

See how he's frowning
And shaking his head
He's never quite happy enough
With his bread

It's too thick, it's too light,
It's too heavy, he'd say,
If only the dough
Would rise faster today.

If only I could work
One hour more
I could sell twice as much
Bread as before

Listen, can you hear
Clara May singing?
So clear and so bright
It's like silver bells ringing

But sadly most days
You don't hear a thing
Because most of the time
Clara May does not sing

You see, Clara refuses
To sing unless
She knows that her voice
Is the one they call best

If only I'd get solo
In the church choir
If only I could sing
One octave higher

If only, if only,
If only could be,
If only, if only,
Then happy I'd be

There's Farmer Brown
Pacing this way and that
My pigs are too thin
My horses too fat

You know I've never
Been one to complain
But if only my fields
Got a little more rain

There's Mr. Mailman
Singing the blues,
If only I had me
A new pair of shoes

There sits a boy
Who wants to be taller
Next door to a woman
Who wants to be smaller

And there sits poor
Little Sara McGoo
Still watching and waiting
For her dream to come true

If that one were thin
If this one not so poor
If only her wallet
Had one dollar more

If only, if only
It's quite clear to see
How the Land of If Only's
Name came to be

See that empty house
To the right,
The one with no mail
The one with no light?

In this house
There used to be
A little girl
Named Kara Lee

Who had one wish
And just one prayer
That she could live
Without this chair

That she'd be given
Just one chance
To spread her arms
Like wings and dance

And so she wished
And so she prayed
Whispering If only
She lived her days

And like her neighbors
And neighbors beside her
She lived a life
That couldn't satisfy her

And then one day
There came a girl
With perfect legs
And a golden curl

Who whispered, Come,
And go with me,
To the place where If Only's
Go to be free

And together they went
Hand in hand
Up over the hill
To the neighboring land

Where the grass is green

Just like ours

Where some days bring sun

And others bring showers

Where some people are short

And some are tall

Some who have much

And some nothing at all

For this land too

Brings days of rain

But people here

Do not complain

Or wish or hope

For that one thing more

But find something

To be thankful for

For the people here

Live for this day

And do not dwell

On yesterday

Or fret about

What might be

They put faith in things

They can not see

For though there's not much
That they can do
To change the road,
They can change the view

And so they live
Simple and free
Not burdened down
By what could be

And that's when
Little Kara Lee
Gripping her chair whispered
What about me?

And so answered
The little girl
With the perfect legs
And the golden curl,

To live here,
You must learn to let go
Of all the If Only's
That burden you so

To never wish
For what you have not
To learn to be happy
For the life you've got

Every day you must

Make a choice

To put a smile on your face

And joy in your voice

Find a way to fill your day

With laughter

And you can stay here

In Happily Ever After

And a smile broke out

On Kara's face

For hope at last

Had found a place

And she closed her eyes

Counted to three

Took all those If Only's

And set them free

And there she lived

And there she stayed

And still she dreamed

And still she prayed

And let go of that

Not meant to be

And at last she lived

Most happily

And that's why in If Only,
That last house to the right,
There sits no mail
And there is no light

We hear someone new
Is about to move in
And, alas, the story
Starts over again

In Happily Ever After
Kara Lee stayed
Until the stars came
To take her away

And now you'll find
On the very best night
When the moon is full
And the stars are bright

If you look way up
Into the sky
You can see Kara Lee
Spread her wings - And fly

For at last
And not by chance
She finally got her wish
…To dance

Are you living in the land of If Only?

If you live burdened
By what could be
And need something
To set you free,

If this is you
Then so I pray
That you would hear me
When I say

Close your eyes
Count to three
Take your If Only's
And set them free

For what will come
Will come despite
Your greatest effort
And your greatest might

And though you can't always
Stop the storm
Or change the road
On which you were born

When you've done all
You know to do
You still have the power
To change your view

Please know you always
Have a choice
To smile through the pain
And put joy in your voice

So in this day may
You choose laughter
And join me in the land
Of Happily Ever After.
kcs

Letters From Readers

Hi Kelly,

My story begins a little more than 10 years ago when I was trying desperately to get pregnant. After 3 1/2 years of trying traditional as well as not so traditional methods, my husband and I decided to go the IVF route. At this time, there wasn't an IVF clinic in Syracuse so we sought out the experts in Rochester, over an hour's drive away. From the start, this process entailed no drinking, exercise, or coffee on the part of the patient and if that wasn't enough to make me cranky...I became a human pin-cushion with daily injections in my thigh and back hip. The first cycle passed with no success. I felt barren, somehow less of a woman. And of course, there was that incessant, annoying, tick, tick, tick of my biological clock in the top of my right ear.

The required time passed and I began my second round of fertility drugs. This time my ovaries responded with a vengeance and I produced a whole soccer team. Yes, there were 14 in all! The plan now was to extract them from my body via vacuum, let them "simmer" for 3 days in the petri-dish and let mother nature....Oh OK, father science, do its thing. The nurse informed me that if any of the eggs fertilized, they would call me and I would drive up early morning of the 4th day to have them/it put back in. WHEW!

Well the call came, it was a Wednesday night and I held my breath as I picked up the phone. Dawn, my assigned nurse, told me I had two viable eggs. TWO!! I danced a little jig in the kitchen and went to tell my husband. His unusual and unsettling response was, OK, but you better get one of your girlfriends to take you because I have a "final" tomorrow morning. At this point, I pictured cutting out his heart and stapling it to his forehead but instead, I calmly replied, can't you reschedule? No, he said, this is very important to me.

Hmmm, I wasn't going to let this get me down, after all I had two viable eggs. It doesn't get any better than that. I called my dear friend Cindy and made arrangements to meet at the Thruway stop in the morning. We arrived at the University of Rochester Hospital and I was excited and anxious. My name was quickly called and I headed straight to the exam room. Dr. Phipps met me, gave me a smile and said my eggs were "Robust." What does that mean, I said? All I could envision were PLUMP eggs. He said that robust eggs were multi-sided with well-matching sides and that the more sides they had, at this point, the better. Well, both my eggs had 8 sides. Can you imagine? Then he proceeded to show my 2 robust eggs up on a screen. WOW! I ran down the hall to get Cindy. She just had to see these eggs. We sat in that exam room and we just stared in awe.

Next, the 2 fertilized eggs made their journey into my body. They then tilted the entire bed downward and told me to relax. No problem....right? I asked them to go and get Cindy. She came back in and I just rubbed my stomach. While I was doing this, I kept repeating, "Lieem," Lieeem (my mantra), implant, implant. After a while, my arm grew tired and Cindy began to rub my belly and say, "Implant, implant."

About a ½ hour passed and I was growing tired of having part of my head in the office plant and asked Cindy to adjust the bed. She turned the knob and suddenly, I was totally upside down. We were both laughing so loud and hard that the nurse came in to see what was going on. She adjusted the bed to a much more comfortable level and we continued rubbing my belly and chanting, "Implant, implant." We left the doctor's later that morning feeling buoyed by such a positive, fun, experience completing this journey. A mere two weeks later, I found out that one of the embryos had implanted and I was pregnant with my first child.

Blessedly Implanted,
Robyn Bombard

Dear Kelly,

Here I am, standing in the middle of my walk-in closet, looking at the rows and rows of shoes lining my shelves. Some of these beauties go back to my early days in NYC, when I was working with one Billie Gordon, top textile stylist in the country. Billie – who had taught me about fine leathers and custom-made shoes that she had me continually return and return in the boxes with the big "F" embossed on them. My devil had worn Ferragamo.

I shook myself back to the present, as I mentally rolled up my sleeves to the daunting task ahead. "Gawd, who are you – Imelda Marcus?!" I chided myself as I taped together the box waiting voraciously to eat the unneeded pairs of blue, purple, red and shiny black leather foot coverings. "What are there, like 1000 pairs?!! Well, maybe 90," I whisper, to no one in particular.

Next to the box is a 2-step step stool, which I'm not quite sure I will be able to balance myself on. Well, best get on with it. So I start to hoist myself up, using the sides of the closet door to steady myself, not wanting to fall. If I did, the cats would not be able to dial 911, and I still hadn't bought one of those thingys for around my neck, "I've fallen and I can't get up".

As if on cue, Michael, the black Alpha male, comes padding into the closet – looking inquisitive: "Whatja doing up there anyway??" he meows. "Later," I tell him, "Mamma's got some closet cleanin' to do."

THE decision had been made a few hours earlier, when I had received a call from my favorite executive search firm in Dallas, TX. Knowing that I had just left my six-figure job at a local Dept. Store, they were eager to make another commission to place me in a comparable position. I had been in the fashion biz for over 23 years; going from Billie's assistant to designing Jaclyn Smith for Kmart to the job as DMM of product development for a southern-based, family-owned chain of better department

---

stores. What she didn't have was some new information that I had just received a month earlier from my orthopedic surgeon.

And now, I had a decision to make. But there really was no decision, was there? I admonished myself. It had been less than two years earlier when I had a spinal fusion that had left me with nerve damage. Damage that I never dreamed would lead to this day. My eyes started to water as a wave of self-pity started to wash over me, remembering the journey from gallivanting all over Europe to...

"NO! You will NOT DO THIS."

"It is what it is - you are not going to wear any of those shoes again. Won't fit over your new fashion accessory!" I look ruefully down at my left leg and foot, encased in a clunky plastic leg brace. Nope, only lace ups and Velcro closings for you, Ms Fashionista! This puppy is permanent!

"Now, where were those glass slippers, Cinderellie?" I thought ruefully as I picked up the stilettos from Florence where I had met the man who I thought was the love of my life – but certainly NOT my Prince Charming - nope, no storybook endings for me. The fashion business was not exactly conducive to long-lasting relationships – a lot like Hollywood, actually. Same fast-paced, mask-wearing sort of business. And a lot of married men took their wedding bands off on the European trips. Why do men do that?!

What I really need is Ruby Red Slippers – yup, that would do the trick all right! There's no place like home, cuz I certainly wasn't in OZ - and needed to just get back to the reality of living my life with a disability. No fairy godmother was going to wave a magic wand, and Scottie was not going to beam me up!

As these thoughts beckoned me into depression once more, I suddenly had a flash of insight, as I saw the leg brace for what it was – a trellis to hold me up as I left behind my old life to embrace the new. Left behind a career that judged people on how they looked instead of who they were inside. Left behind a childhood dream of becoming a world-renowned fashion designer to embrace my path as an adult, honed by experience and pain. A path that would allow me, as a spiritual teacher, to help others realize they could be more than they ever thought they could be, and to love themselves just as they were. Not a curse, but a blessing, helping me to stand and wear shoes that really fit me – not a false image of who I needed to be. I was going to be fine - just fine!

With renewed resolve, I climbed up onto the second step of the stool, scooping the first row of shoes into the box. As they clattered into their new transport, my mind flashed onto the blue-and-white plastic parking sticker that the Dr. had bestowed upon me and I laughed – well, at least I get Rock-Star parking!

Rebecca Nagy, The Mind Maven ™, is an inspirational speaker and spiritual teacher living in Charlotte, NC. The above story is taken from her upcoming book, Standing On Your Own, which is due out in late 2009. A member of The National Speakers Association, she speaks about how Your Thoughts Can Change Your Life: Meditation for Health and Focus and Spirit in the Workplace. For more information: www.rebeccanagy.com

---

Dear Kelly,

My 85-year-old mother was in the hospital for breast cancer surgery. I had been greatly concerned about her dementia, but now this. Sitting with her during the night following surgery, I thought this was the end of the world. I felt alone and helpless.

I decided to listen to a recording that I brought with me. I put on the headphones and started the tape. The humorous stories I heard were so comforting that I experienced a renewal. It was a recording made by some of my friends during a storytelling concert in the park. Hearing their voices gave me even more comfort for it seemed they were there with me. Now feeling calm and peaceful, I was able to sleep *in spurts, or between my mother's fits of restlessness. I made certain the nurses were doing their best to care for her.*

My dad and sister were quiet and glum the following day and I could stand it no longer. I pulled out a pair of Groucho Marx glasses and nose, with a mustache. I put them on. This broke the darkness in the room and we all began to laugh aloud; even my mother. Soon she was wearing them, bringing laughter to all hospital staff that walked into the room. All in all, my "strange fit of humor" brightened many hearts that day.

Sylvia Payne

www.storytraditions.com

Kelly,

Girl, my fairy tale has been hijacked so many times I can't count that high anymore. The most memorable one was also the most preventable one. When I married my second ex-husband, "Scum Dog" in 1989, his family gushed all over me at the reception. They circled me like a pack of vultures vying for 3-day-old road-kill! Each and every one of them said a variation of this:

"How did 'Larry' (name changed to protect the perpetually guilty) find and marry a sweet schoolteacher like you? You're just what he needs to straighten up."

At the time the words "straighten up" didn't mean anything to me, but on the first night of our honeymoon at Hilton Head, their words began to haunt me. "Larry" vanished in the middle of the night when he thought I was asleep. The sound of the door closing woke me up. There was no "Larry" in the suite, no "Larry" on the beach...or car in the parking lot. He sneaked back into the room at dawn with a lame excuse.

"I couldn't sleep," he said, "so I took a drive."

I heard that excuse each night during our honeymoon. When we returned home, I put my private-eye hat on and went to work. I began calling his friends to see what they could tell me about his odd behavior. His oldest friends confessed that "Larry" had been doing drugs since he was sixteen, and that his addiction had gotten worse over time. I'll say! Further snooping turned up tiny bags of white power.

Now I knew exactly what the phrase "straighten up" meant! You're right, Kelly. I had married a man with a monkey on his back. Not only had I married him, but the charming devil had convinced me to quit my teaching job and go into business with him. So, there I was, married and in business with an addict.

The first year, I insisted on rehab. The second year I began planning how to parachute off my hijacked plane and deal with closing the business. It took a lot of time to orchestrate. The third year, I asked Scum Dog for an unusual anniversary gift: a battery-operated screwdriver. Hmmmm.

A short time later, after meetings with lawyers about the business, district attorneys about his criminal activities, and a few friends who volunteered for bodyguard duty, I put my "exit stage right" strategy into action. I had my nails done bright red and cruised through K-Mart to buy new dead bolts. Yes, you're right! I used my anniversary gift, the battery-operated screwdriver, to change the locks. Then I threw his clothes on the sidewalk and went to wash my hands. I had my nail painted red so he would see me giving him the finger from the other side of the locked door.

That was the longest, scariest 2.8 years of my life. It was also the time when I learned the most about myself. I found out that I'm a survivor with one wicked sense of humor!

Myelita Melton

Myelita Melton, CEO
SpeakEasy Communications, Inc.
Tel: 704-662-9424
Cell: 704-516-5945

Dear Kelly,

I remember when one of my best girlfriends got dumped by a guy she really cared for. He had given her a stuffed teddy bear on the first date, and we took that bear and beat the crap out of it. Removed an eye and,ripped out some of the stuffing before throwing it into the big garbage can. Not fun for the little guy, but we laughed so hard through the whole thing it was cathartic.

"C" in California

Dear Kelly,

Having grown up in a family with four children I always dreamed of having a large family of my own. I envisioned myself at the helm of the mini van blazing a trail back and forth to school and soccer practice while the kids poked at each other in the backseat. We would sing songs, play car bingo and count cows. At home we'd play games, make chocolate chip cookies and drink hot cocoa. And every night, just before bedtime, we'd read together. Our home would be filled with love and laughter. Now in my early 40s I realize that I may never have a large family of my own. And although I may not drive a mini van, my home is filled with laughter and love, I still sing in the car, bake chocolate chip cookies and drink hot cocoa.

Susanne Gaddis, PhD, CSP
The Communications Doctor
Professional Speaker and Executive Coach

www.CommunicationsDoctor.com

Kelly,

Today is the fifth anniversary of my father-in-law's passing. My father-in-law was in the hospital, in the end stages of COPD. My wife was his caregiver and while I was working for IBM at the time, I was commuting between Chicago and the farm in S.C. While in the hospital, my father-in-law tried to still give my wife orders about how to run the farm.

Every morning, my wife would wake up, tell the farmhand what had to be done, fed the dogs and drove 2 hours in to Charleston to spend time with her dad. Now the farmhand, Mack, wasn't the most reliable guy. Over the years, my father-in-law had to call the sheriff and a local judge to get Mack out of jail for some reason or another. At times, my father-in-law threatened to fire Mack.

One day while Mack was using the tractor to pull a stump out of a field, one of our dogs Dottie jumped in. I grabbed one of the disposable cameras that was lying around, ran over and took a picture of Dottie in the cab. I then got the film developed.

The next day, while at the hospital, we told her dad that we had to fire Mack. The expression on his face was a mix of anger, shock, and disgust. Since he couldn't talk, his eyes said it all... "What did Mack do now !?!" We told him not to worry, we found a perfect replacement. Again a bit of a shock. Trying to get a good farmhand was next to impossible. We then showed him the picture of Dottie in the tractor cab and he rolled his eyes and laughed.

He made us put the picture up so he could look at it all the time. Dottie became one of his favorite dogs because she would escape from the pens and sleep on a box in front of his window. She always found a way to make him smile and laugh. Sometimes it's the little things in life that make it all worthwhile.

Michael Segel

Dear Kelly,

How do I even begin to describe how humor has saved me throughout life? Having a child with special needs, humor was about all I had left to keep me sane – and to communicate with my child – for when everything else failed to reach her, humor is what she reacted to most. When I could make her laugh, I knew I had reached deep inside of her somehow and for that one moment, things felt normal.

I remember when our second child came along and my special-needs child went into the hospital (again) and things went crazy. My husband was at the hospital around the clock; I was taking care of a brand new baby and freaking out because I couldn't be with my child at the hospital. A friend came over, finally, to take care of the baby and I jumped in the car and rushed over to the hospital. My husband, who had not been updated, came out groggy and bleary-eyed to meet me in the parking lot and went around to get the baby out. Empty seat. He immediately starts screaming, "Where's the baby! You forgot the baby!" And for the first time, I saw an opportunity to FINALLY pull one over on my husband, who is usually the trickster. "Oh my gosh!" I screamed. "I forgot the baby!" That did it – I finally got him. And I still laugh about it to this day.

Occasionally we would go on trips for work (not very often for obvious reasons) and we could never find people to take care of Amanda, so we used to leave her with this robust woman named Erma who took her to church with her, because Erma went to church all the time and would never miss church. We were never sure what happened there, but we were so happy to have someone take care of her, we didn't care. All the other parents kept calling their sitters – not us! We still laugh about those times and about hearing that the woman had fed our daughter cornbread when our daughter couldn't even swallow.

We never slept. And we broke out into Barney show tunes at random moments because that's all our daughter would ever watch. From the moment we found out Amanda was special, our life completely changed. We didn't have a choice.

We had to redefine normal. I always believed that God would want me to be happy with this situation. Some people would think God hated them for giving them such a huge portion of crap. But I didn't think that way. I think God gives you what your strength can handle. I thought I was strong before, but now that she has died – I realize that I'm having to find an even greater strength. Funny, but I would gladly go back to how it was, even on the most miserable of days, just to have her back again.

I always say to myself, "Be careful, because there can be an 'even worse' to this too." You never really face the worst – and you learn to be happy with what you've got. And you learn to surround yourself with positive people – that's key!

Janis K
(P.S. A drink every now and then helps too)

Dear Kelly,

I was a stay-at-home Mom with a preschool son and daughter. I practically jumped on my husband every evening when he returned from work hungry for a conversation in complete sentences. But he, unfortunately, had spent the day talking and was ready to chill. One afternoon I had watched a talk show interview with an author who had written 101 ways to say I Love You. She shared all kinds of ideas for wives. That day when my husband came home I was chatty Cathy bursting with something different to talk about. I shared several suggestions with him, one of which was to stand naked in the coat closet wrapped in Saran Wrap, so when he came home and hung up his coat - TA DA! There you'd be, gift-wrapped and gorgeous.

Weeks went by and I forgot all about the show. My Mom was visiting us and my husband went to bed, leaving us time to have some girl talk. When time came for us to call it a day, I went into our bedroom, glanced over at the bed to see my husband bundled under the covers sleeping. I sat down on the edge of the bed with my back to him to take off my shoes and socks. That's when I heard the closet door creaaaaak, and slooowly open. First I froze. My thoughts were, "If my husband is in bed behind me, and my mother is in her room, then WHO IS COMING OUT OF THE CLOSET????" And there the man stood in front of me, naked as a jaybird. I freaked! I screamed and totally came unglued. He sat down beside me, put his arm around me, and said, "Honey, I'm so sorry, I didn't mean to scare you, was just trying to say 'I love you.' " He hadn't forgotten the show. I haven't forgotten that night. The best part was explaining it all to my mother.

Sometimes we can take ourselves too seriously, give ourselves bad grades as wives and Moms and forget we have a choice about what we spend our thoughts on. For a change, try thinking about what's working in your life instead of dwelling on what isn't. Most likely you couldn't fix it anyway.

Denise Tolton

Kelly:

I still remember when our house burned down. We were at my neighbor's house and my brother-in-law, Shawn, was there. Shawn asked me if there had been eggs at my house. I said yes. He asked if there had been bacon. I said yes. "What about bread?" he asks. I said yes. "Well, let's go," he said. "I'd say breakfast is ready."

I also used to give my husband a hard time for having the nerve to have a heart attack two weeks before we were moving. I told him it was a heck of a way to get out of helping!

Cheryl

11892325R0011